Let the Mountains Talk,
Let the Rivers Run

Let the Mountains Talk, Let the Rivers Run

A CALL TO SAVE THE EARTH

David Brower
with Steve Chapple

Foreword by Amory Lovins

Sierra Club Books
San Francisco

The Sierra Club, founded in 1892 by John Muir, has devoted itself to the study and protection of the earth's scenic and ecological resources—mountains, wetlands, woodlands, wild shores and rivers, deserts and plains. The publishing program of the Sierra Club offers books to the public as a nonprofit educational service in the hope that they may enlarge the public's understanding of the Club's basic concerns. The point of view expressed in each book, however, does not necessarily represent that of the Club. The Sierra Club has some sixty chapters throughout the United States. For information about how you may participate in its programs to preserve wilderness and the quality of life, please address inquiries to Sierra Club, 85 Second Street, San Francisco, California 94105, or visit our website at www.sierraclub.org.

Published by Sierra Club Books
85 Second Street, San Francisco, CA 94105
www.sierraclub.org/books

Produced and distributed by
University of California Press
Berkeley and Los Angeles, California
University of California Press, Ltd.
London, England
www.ucpress.edu

SIERRA CLUB, SIERRA CLUB BOOKS, and the Sierra Club design logos
are registered trademarks of the Sierra Club.

Library of Congress Cataloging-in-Publication Data is available
on request from Sierra Club Books.
ISBN: 978-1-57805-138-0

Originally published in hardcover in 1995 by HarperCollins Publishers, New York. First published in paperback in 2000 by New Society Publishers, British Columbia, Canada.

Book design by George Brown
Cover design by Linda Herman
Cover photograph of David Brower © Kurt Markus

Printed in the United States of America on New Leaf Ecobook 50 acid-free paper, which contains a minimum of 50 percent post-consumer waste, processed chlorine free. Of the balance, 25 percent is certified by the Forest Stewardship Council to contain no old-growth trees and to be pulped totally chlorine free.

12 11 10 09 08 07
10 9 8 7 6 5 4 3 2 1

To those already committed to healing the Earth,
and to those about to be

Contents

Acknowledgments

WE WOULD LIKE TO THANK a number of people for taking time to share their thoughts in the middle of busy days and nights: Sam LaBudde, Jimmy Langman, John Knox, Justin Lowe, and Gar Smith of the Earth Island Institute; John Berger, Paul Hawken, Garrett DeBell, Amory Lovins, Kenneth Brower, Peter Warshall, Thomas Rymsza, Huey Johnson; Bob Ekey, communications director of the Greater Yellowstone Coalition, and Peter Aengst; Randy Hayes, director of the Rainforest Action Network; Michael Oppenheimer, senior scientist for the Environmental Defense Fund; Thomas J. Cassidy, general counsel, American Rivers; Mark Dowie, Richard Parker, and Will Nixon.

We are grateful to Quincey Tompkins Imhoff, executive director of the Foundation for Deep Ecology; Alfred Heller; and Thomas Wynett, for their generous financial support.

Chapple, especially, is thankful for the deadline indulgences of Karin Evans and Terry McDonnell; the hospitality of Bea Vogel,

Gil Bagot, Jr., Patti Bartlett, David and Isis Schwartz, David Helvarg and Nancy Ledansky; the good love of Kent McCarthy for Anchor Bay; and the usual extreme kindness shown by Maria Ines Pentagna Salgado, Cody, and Jack to his line of work.

Finally, this book would not have come about without the encouragement of Joann Moschella, editor of HarperCollins West, and Mikhail Davis, director of the Brower Fund; the precise pencil of Lisa Zuniga Carlsen; and the instincts of our agents, Ellen Levine and Anne Dubuisson.

Publisher's Note

SINCE THE LAST EDITION of this book appeared, Dave
Brower left the Earth, followed not long after by his wife,
Anne. But if he is no longer "the greatest living environmentalist,"
as Amory Lovins describes him a few pages on, his voice remains
among the most powerful to speak for the planet during the last
century, and his legacy of conservation achievements will—with
our help—live well beyond this century. Dave had no opportunity
to update information from earlier editions of this book, or to add
new material on environmental challenges and innovative solutions that have emerged recently, as he surely would have done.
Readers should be aware of this but understand that it matters little, for his memories are just as vividly recalled, his arguments just
as passionate and pertinent, as they were when he and Steve Chapple first set them down in the early 1990s. We offer them to readers
and activists of the next generation, who will need them as they
take up his work of Earth-saving.

Foreword
Amory Lovins

SOME WISE BIOLOGIST, perhaps E. O. Wilson, remarked
that bees, ants, and termites, though not very smart individually,
display much intelligence collectively—while people are just the
opposite. Yet now and then the search for intelligent life on Earth
turns up a promising specimen—a much higher primate who, by
combined force of logic and love, humor and passion, awakens
the rest of us to our personal and especially our collective
potential for enriching our habitat and each other.

Such a rare creature is David Brower, the greatest living
environmentalist, among the greatest of all time—our generation's Thoreau or Emerson or Muir. His unique achievements are
mainly described in terms of wilderness saved, lively organizations created in fifty-odd countries, laws passed, attitudes
changed, people inspired, publications issued, careers nurtured.
Author Jerry Mander calls him "the most visionary, effective, and
inspiring environmentalist of our age.... [I]t was his brand of no-
compromise activism and thinking that has essentially vaulted the

ecology movement into becoming a major international force." All correct, all incomplete. But those of us fortunate to have learned for decades from this master of natural philosophy and effective action, seasoned by his half-century at the forefront of the global movement, are also especially happy to see the ripe and subtle wisdom of his eighty-eight years distilled into this book.

Before he led the building of the modern American, and indeed the global, environmental movement—the most obvious expression of his life's work—Dave's range of gifts emerged from equally diverse and complex challenges. As the eyes for his blind mother, he became a naturalist and aesthetician devoted to "mystery, the unending search for truth, the truth of beauty." As a leading mountaineer and co-inventor of ski mountaineering, he honed native boldness seasoned by judgment. As a soldier in World War II, rising in combat from private to major in the Tenth Mountain Division, he mastered leadership and organization. As an editor, he evolved clarity and grace. All these experiences, and more, fitted him to keep the gift moving, giving strategy and stamina to the thousands he continues to guide, instruct, and inspire.

We first met in London in 1969, when Philip Howell Evans—the great unsung Welsh landscape photographer—and I were advised by *National Geographic* to send our atmospheric mountain photographs to Dave because "he likes this sort of thing." Long in awe of his stunningly beautiful Exhibit Format books, which shaped our generation's appreciation of wild places, we hesitantly did so, hoping for the favor of a little advice. He liked our work, asking for more and for some writing. What a shock it was when at our next meeting, he gave us a half-hour to decide whether, over the next two months, we wanted to create one of his "big books." We'd never written, or photographed for, a book. He said it was time we started. He wanted me to do not only the writing but also the layout. I said I'd never done that. He said it was time I learned. He was right. The resulting book, *Eryri, the Mountains of Longing*, helped save a British national park from despoliation by the world's largest mining company. The company never took our efforts to improve its financial performance in quite the gracious spirit in which they were meant, but did back off. Three decades later, having achieved mutual respect, we're exploring how to work together to make the firm a natural capitalist (www.naturalcapitalism.org).

Working with Dave on the book was a world-class graduate seminar in just about everything. Academic research was less interesting and far less important. Anyhow, Oxford wouldn't let me do a doctorate in energy policy—which, two years before the 1973 oil embargo, wasn't considered an academic subject; they had no chair in it. (They do now.) In 1971, moved by Dave's vision, I resigned from academia to work for him full-time—ultimately for a decade in London and another three years in the United States, earning about enough to pay the phone bill, but with complete freedom to choose tasks, priorities, and methods. All that mattered was quality, integrity, and results.

It was an adventure. We'd meet all over the world—in all-night strategy sessions, in airports, before congressional committees, wherever. When Dave was coming to town, the proper equipment for going to see him included a toothbrush and passport, because there was no telling what airplane I'd be whisked aboard to go address the critical issue of the day. In those days, Friends of the Earth was largely a collection of talented people Dave had recruited, supported (too often from his own meager pocket), and given the freedom to do what they did best. The style was so far from bureaucratic as to verge on anarchic; the results were exceptional; the feeling was exhilarating; all became addictive.

My parents, I later discovered, were worried about my giving up an academic career, but they kindly kept it to themselves. It didn't matter. I'd entered a far more demanding and rewarding course of study and action, requiring one to pick up a couple of new disciplines a year. The final exam was effectiveness. I learned to do now what is necessary and important, how to influence others with diverse views and values, how things work, and what matters. Over the past half-century, hundreds if not thousands of young people have followed similar paths, joining this mentor who is at once charismatic and reflective, funny and profound. His commitment and personal interest have moved us all to give up safe, conventional, well-paying but unrewarding career tracks and to join his movement to save the world. That process continues unabated to this day as Dave continues to attract and enlist the talented youngsters who will strive to fill his giant shoes.

On rare occasions, we'd disagree about tactics, but I gradually learned that Dave was right; he was simply thinking ten years further ahead. He retains that uncanny prescience to this day. Still the most brilliantly visionary person I know, perpetually a decade or more ahead, he's asking and starting to answer the key questions that haven't yet occurred to the rest of us.

Dry humor falls like gentle rain through his speaking and writing. It's self-deprecatory, often with a sting in the tail but never unkind. He has learned, as the environmental movement needs to learn, not to take itself too seriously. The underlying passion is still there too, but now more tolerantly accepting of mistakes (which are, as Edwin Land reminded us, "events not yet fully turned to one's advantage"). A few facts change, of course— the Hypercar™ described in this book is already starting to move into the marketplace (www.hypercarcenter.org)—but the underlying principles are perennial. Dave's insight into the majesties of life and the follies of politics is like a fine vintage, mellowing with age. The innate curiosity, optimism, risk-friendliness, and joie de vivre remain extraordinary. And the fine hand of Dave's wife, Anne, also a brilliant editor, shines through the insights and the language.

In short, readers are in for a treat—for the privilege of learning why and how to commit themselves irrevocably to the brave and necessary agenda of global restoration. As the twenty-first century begins, it's too early to tell whether the recent upstart experiment of combining opposable thumbs with a large forebrain will turn out to be a good idea, but this book offers hope that it may. By leading what is now the global movement to sustain life, David Brower has already changed a myriad lives. This book could change yours, and hence those of all beings on Earth.

Old Snowmass, Colorado

February 5, 2000

CPR *for the* Earth:
An Invitation

I WAS STANDING beside Lester Brown, president of
the World Watch Institute, watching him sign copies of his
latest book at a store in Washington, D.C. Lester is a hero of mine.
In his early days as an agronomist in India, he once saved 10 million people from starving to death. He foresaw a crop failure and
was able to get the United States to ship one-fifth of its wheat
crop to avert the famine. That's something. On this day, he suddenly turned and asked me if I knew who had come up with the
quotation his publisher had put on the book's jacket: "We do not
inherit the Earth from our fathers, we are borrowing it from our
children."

"I have no idea," I replied.

"Those words," said Lester, "are carved in stone at the
National Aquarium, and your name is underneath them."

I was a bit pleased and thoroughly puzzled.

At home in California, I searched my unorganized files to find out when I could have said those words. I stumbled upon the answer in the pages of an interview that had taken place in a North Carolina bar so noisy, I could only marvel that I was heard at all. Possibly, I didn't remember saying it because by then they had me on my third martini.

I decided the words were too conservative for me. We're not borrowing from our children, we're *stealing* from them—and it's not even considered to be a crime.

Let that be my epitaph, when I need it.

In the years since the Industrial Revolution, we humans have been partying pretty hard. We've ransacked most of the Earth for resources. A small part of the world's population wound up with some nice goodies, but now we're eating the seed corn. We are living off the natural capital of the planet, the principal, and not the interest. The soil, the seas, the forests, the rivers, and the protective atmospheric cover—all are being depleted. It was a grand binge, but the hangover is now upon us, and it will soon be throbbing.

To our unborn children, it will seem that we did, indeed, burn books to get light, burn furniture to run air-conditioning, and burn arbors to warm ourselves. For a while it worked. We did multiply and subdue the Earth. Our children will credit us for that, but they must face the fact that the Earth is not theirs to subdue, but rather to cherish. There is only one Earth.

The solution is simple: We must go back to the world's ravaged places and bind up the wounds we've inflicted. We must do our best to restore the natural world to something like it was 200 years ago, before we monkeywrenched nature. We must redesign our cities at the same time. Otherwise, we are out of here.

I believe this to be the most important challenge we face on Earth. Old, tired, me-first thinking won't do it. There is still time for the contrivers in America to come up with a better answer before the harm becomes irreparable.

WHILE I WAS WRITING this book, I attended my first Grateful Dead concert. I was invited by Dead musician Bob Weir, who had attended my eighty-second birthday party. The first thing I thought as I surveyed the crowd of 22,000 swaying twenty-four-year-olds was that my presence would bring the average age up to at least twenty-four and a half.

Then I wondered what wilderness experience would be left for these young people. What sort of a planet were we—members of my generation, and those quavering kids in their fifties and sixties, too—bequeathing? I thought of what I would say to these people if I could play Grateful Dead piano instead of semi-classical. What sort of speech might I give? It would have to be a short one. Maybe I would begin:

"While you are listening to this wonderful music that crosses so many boundaries, we are getting rid of the things worth crossing boundaries for. One of the most important things left on the

Earth for you is wilderness. Your minds, your bodies, the 100,000 chemical reactions that go on inside you without your knowing, the ability to hear the Dead in stereo, all were formed in wilderness, during the 4 billion years of life on this Earth: not in so-called civilization, not in the last two hundred years since the Industrial Revolution, but in wilderness. There have been no mistakes. You are here.

"There are things you can do to make life better," I would say, "to fix the Earth. If you don't do it, it won't get done. That wilderness within you and without you won't be there." Maybe there'd be a little foot shuffling at this point, so I'd remind them, "Hey, I'm an elder. You've got to listen to me. It took me a long time to become one. It won't take you that long. I'm sorry to give you the bad news, but you're going to be as old as I am much sooner than you think."

If that didn't get a laugh, I'd say, "I know, there's this problem with the environmental movement. It's like the problem of the Bible. There's no humor in it. I would say, Whatever you do, don't violate Rule Number 6. What is Rule Number 6? Rule Number 6 says, Never take yourself too seriously. (Of course, I do, but I pretend I don't.) What are the other rules? There are no other rules."

Most of these young people were probably gainfully employed. I would say to them, "Put some eco-spin into your job description—whatever you do in life, make sure to include CPR for the Earth. The Earth is a living throbbing organism. It needs CPR—Conservation-Preservation-Restoration—on a regular basis:

"*Conservation:* We've got to use our resources rationally. We haven't been all that rational these last brief millennia.

"*Preservation:* We've got to preserve what we can never replace. That's what wilderness is. That's what biodiversity is, and we're getting rid of both faster than anybody has ever done.

"*Restoration:* We're bright enough to build back, to restore the rivers we've dammed, the forests we've clearcut, the seas we've bloodied, polluted, and strip-mined with drift nets; the mountains we've bolted and bulldozed, the deserts we've spoiled or mistakenly created; the ozone layer we've punctured. We can't restore a lot of things that are gone, but we can certainly restore human integrity."

That's a little heavy. I wouldn't want to lose my audience. I would quickly add, "You have opportunities. Seize them."

Then I might think, Maybe these young people have never even seen a wilderness the way I have been privileged to, countless times. So I would add, "If this amphitheater were a wilderness and you were all here, it wouldn't be a wilderness anymore. Just a few of you should come to the wilderness at one time. And bring your music. Not just to listen, but to create some yourself. Learn to hear the music of the Earth."

Maybe someone heckles me: "Music like what!"

"Like the sound of a small stream," I would reply. "Like a canyon wren trilling down the scale in counterpoint. Dam that stream? It's your choice. Quell that bird, if you dare. But ask yourself what your grandchildren will ask you: What was it like, that *music?*"

I would still be tempted to tell them about a few of my own favorite places, but I would have to say, "This information is classified. If you want to know more about the places I really like to go, let's go out and close a bar."

After the Dead are done, of course.

THAT WAS my fantasy. In real life, Bob Weir came up to me backstage and asked where he could get my sweatshirt, which said across the chest: "Free Al Gore." Bob told me that he was a friend of the vice president, and would be meeting with him in a couple of weeks.

"You've got it," I said.

I like Al Gore. I thought *Earth In the Balance* was one of the best books written by someone close to the American presidency since Theodore Roosevelt lost his comeback as leader of the Bull Moose Party. There are some things I disagree with in that book, but certainly a thinking man with children and heart wrote it.

One of the biggest disappointments of my life is that the movement to conserve, preserve, and restore the Earth is so absent from the legislative and political arena, which is like trying to walk in a wheelchair. The speed with which we are losing the Earth is devastating, and must be reversed, fast. We supporters of the environmental movement need to support the U-turn.

What I want to know is, did Al Gore get my sweatshirt and wear it to a cabinet meeting or photo opportunity? If he did, maybe things will change a little. Rule Number 6, remember.

IN THIS BOOK, let me share with you some visions of how we can make our children proud of the paradise they will inherit. Let's remember how the Earth looked just a few hundred years ago, and let's talk about how our Earth ought to look in another hundred or so years from now. Let's talk about pelicans and tigers, bristlecone pines and hypercars, mountains and CPR for the Earth.

It will be an adventure to share together.

PART I

Opportunities

CHAPTER I

Seeing and Remembering

We are confronted with insurmountable opportunities.

—Pogo

MY FRIEND Ansel Adams, the photographer of Yosem-
ite, said, "If you're going to get old, get as old as you can get." A
few years ago, when I was seventy-seven, I asked To Whom It
May Concern for a twenty-year extension. To quote George
Burns, in whose reckoning I must be a teenager, "Shoot for 100.
Very few people die after that." I say, borrow time without compunction: There is plenty of time later to be dead.

When you're my age, you think you're an oracle and that people had better listen to you. In fact, they sometimes seem to like to.

Life can begin at eighty, but you don't need to wait that long.

MY EARLIER LIFE began in 1912 beside the tracks of the Atche-
son, Topeka, and Santa Fe in Berkeley, California. My earliest
memory is of my brother, three years old, standing in his bed,

silhouetted against the headlight of an oncoming railroad loco-motive as it roared past our bedroom. I was six months old. Whoever doesn't believe this is invited to disprove it.

When I was nine, in 1921, I remember traveling in a Maxwell touring car up the old one-lane dirt road to Lake Tahoe, in the Sierra. It took three days to get there. We camped well be-yond Colfax, in a forest of mixed pine and fir. Right away, I went exploring and I found a spring. I knew what a spring was because my father, an instructor of descriptive geometry at the Univer-sity of California, had shown me one in the hills behind campus, not far beyond where the first cyclotron would later be built. I was quite pleased to find clear water bubbling from dirt.

The next summer we drove back up to Tahoe and over to Donner Lake, where the early immigrants had met such misfor-tune, and we stopped at the same campsite where I had discov-ered the spring. It was gone. The forest all around it was gone.

Two years before that Sierra spring was clearcut, I became the eyes for my mother. She had lost her sight right after the birth of my younger brother. The cause was an inoperable brain tumor. When she regained her strength, she was first guided on a walk of two blocks to church. Then she got bold, and I got bold, and together we walked from our house, about 200 feet above sea level, to Grizzly Peak—at 1,759 feet, it was the second-highest point in our Berkeley Hills.

It was a joyful thing, that first big walk. It was my job to tell my mother where to put her feet in the rough places, and which one, right or left, but there was no great worry. She was a country girl, my mother, in her early forties and strong. She liked to be outdoors. Even blind, she felt good about it. At the top, I described the vista for her: the hills; the galaxy of flowers; the few new houses; a red-tailed hawk floating on the wind, looking for field mice; the fog coming over San Francisco Bay; the glimpse of the open sea through the Golden Gate. There was no Golden Gate Bridge, no Bay Bridge, so many fewer people in San Francisco, Oakland, San Jose, and Marin. We didn't have all the gas-powered vehicles then. We hadn't manufactured all that smog.

I THINK NOW that those loggers who destroyed my spring, and the Forest Service that served them, went about their work with the same dedication as a whaler hunting down the last blue whale. It was their livelihood, those loggers, their lifestyle, their art. But it is *our* future.

I think too about all the wild beauty I saw for my mother, and the destruction of that beauty that I've seen for myself. When this unsustainable orgy of cutting and running is finally over, the logger, like the buffalo hunter, like the whaler, will exist only in storybooks. I believe it will come true, and in your lifetime.

It would be too easy, however, to blame the destruction of the Earth's forests on those men who logged my cherished spring, or on a few misguided scientists. We have all played a role by belonging to a society that judges its worth by the quantity of what it consumes. By not remembering, by refusing to see.

I have seen a lot go right in my eighty-two years on the planet, but I've also seen a lot go wrong. In my lifetime the world has used up four times the resources it used in all previous history. The population of the Earth has tripled, to what some ecologists think is about ten times the number the planet is capable of sustaining, given what we have chewed up so far. By 2010 it is expected to double again. Humans are far too fertile and over-consuming, especially in the North. Good breeding has been overdone.

Since that moment when I stood describing for my mother the view over the waters of San Francisco Bay, we've lost more than half of our native redwoods. Only 4 percent of the original stand is left. Some remain in Muir Woods, just below Mount Tamalpais, across the bay from where we stood. There used to be 6,000 miles of good salmon streams in California's Central Valley. Now we're down to about 200, and people are arguing over how much water the endangered salmon should be allowed to be endangered in. Only eighty years ago there were no dams on the mighty Columbia River. Now there are many dams, and the salmon don't like it.

There are too many dams on the Snake River, as well as on the Frazier, the Sacramento, and the San Joaquin. There's just a piddling left for those salmon, and those that make it over the fish ladders to spawn. Once they hatch, the few young salmon must then swim miles through slack water, survive turbines, and, if they make it to the ocean, they must contend with drift-netters on the high seas—the buffalo hunters of our time.

As for the inexhaustible sacred cod of the Grand Banks, they are all but gone. Imagine. It has taken five centuries, but they have become like the passenger pigeon. Forty to one hundred species of plant or animal life disappear every day—nobody knows how many for sure.

As entire mosaics of green ecosystems disappear, so, too, do the birds—three decades after Rachel Carson wrote *Silent Spring*. We won some good battles on behalf of the eagle and the peregrine, but the DDT that once weakened the shells of their eggs is still cheaply available in developing countries. Seventy percent of the bird species in the world are in decline, and about 1,000 face extinction.

As the protective ozone layer of our planet thins, we suspect that the increased radiation is killing off toads and frogs in America's Sierra and Cascades. In Australia, billboards proclaim the danger to fair-skinned humans; and cats, whose sunburned ears have been removed in hopes that skin cancer will not metastasize, sadly walk Australia's gardens and streets.

In Florida, alligators are born with small and malformed penises. In Britain, male trout, under the mistaken hormonal impression that they are females, are producing albumen for eggs they will never form. The industrialized world is awash in a sea of estrogens. These estrogens, most chemically derived, are believed to originate in certain plastics and from the pollution of our clean water, and the implications are not good for the males of our own species, who have in the United States experienced a twofold increase in prostate cancer in recent decades; Denmark and other European countries have seen a threefold increase in cancer of the testes.

When I was a boy, water was cleaner. It should be more so now. But you can't purify water with additives.

What happened? Sometimes we have been greedy and unthinking, but at other times the road to environmental disaster has been paved with good intentions. Too often in what we do, we fail to consider the two most important things: the cost to the future, and the cost to the Earth. We can be very clever, we humans, but sometimes not so smart.

In Egypt, the Nile River had been doing just fine for millennia, annually flooding its banks with life-giving nutrients, which made early agriculture possible and later fed an immense sardine fishery in the Mediterranean. Then Russia rushed to help dam the Nile at Aswân, to provide hydroelectric power. In my lifetime no more crazy things have been done than in the mad dash for more energy, and the way we use it. These days, the sardines in the Mediterranean are dead and gone, and Egypt's farmers are not so happy, either. Now the Nile offers not good soil but crop-weakening salts. In some of the new warm irrigation ditches, a parasite that lives in the snails has infected three-quarters of the human population with schistosomiasis, and it is not a nice disease.

In America, we stopped man's hubris in the Grand Canyon of the Colorado River, one of the planet's most sublime chasms. There the battle was fought and won in the name of Beauty. They wanted to dam the waters.

I was then the first executive director of the Sierra Club. We put full-page ads in the *New York Times*, *Washington Post*, and other papers and magazines. One of my favorites ran in *Scientific American* and asked: "Should We Also Flood the Sistine Chapel So Tourists Can Get Nearer the Ceiling?" The ads—augmented by strenuous lobbying, thousands of letters and phone calls, two books, and two films—helped kill the dam. One ad also ended the tax-deductible status of the Sierra Club. In fact, the U.S. Internal Revenue Service, which may have been less subtle in those days, ended our eco-innocence (tax-deductible income) that very day, when the director of the IRS met over drinks with one angry and powerful congressman, who is now a friend of mine. Times change.

In just the twenty-five years since the first Earth Day, that magnificent outpouring of awareness, we have reduced enough forests around the world to cover the United States from the Mississippi to the Atlantic seaboard, north to south. We've created enough desert to equal all the cropland in China. We've lost enough soil by other means—pavement and condominiums, wind and water erosion, inundation, and poorly informed application of chemicals—to equal all the cropland in India. That's one-seventh of the world's productive land lost since Earth Day began. And in that time our population doubled.

The enormity of what we are doing must come to pervade our thinking. Our religions haven't quite prepared us for our current situation.

I was once at a conference where the aim was to expose Presbyterians to an environmentalist. A minister said Man was

co-creator, with God, of the Earth. Anybody who thinks he is a
co-creator with God is having a little trouble with humility.
Why would God pick something that came along so very recently to be in His image? I realized we were probably the most
arrogant species that had ever arrived on Earth, as well as the
Johnny-come-latelies of evolution. It occurred to me then that
should we squeeze the age of the Earth down to six days of bibli-
cal creation, we would get a time line something like this (and
not a few people have repeated my thought):

Sunday at midnight, the Earth is created. There is no life
until Tuesday noon. Millions upon millions of species come during the week, and millions of species go. By Saturday morning at
seven, there's been enough chlorophyll manufactured for the fossil fuels to begin to form. Around four in the afternoon, the great
reptiles come on stage. They hang around for a long time, as
species go, until nine-thirty, a five-hour run. The Grand Canyon
begins taking shape eighteen minutes before midnight. Nothing
like us shows up for another fifteen minutes. No Homo sapiens
until thirty seconds ago. Let the party begin! A second and a half
back, we throw the habits of hunting and gathering to the winds,
and learn to change the environment to suit our appetites. We
get rid of everything we can't eat as fast as we possibly can, and
that's the beginning of agriculture.

A third of a second before midnight, Buddha; a quarter of a
second, Jesus Christ; a fortieth of a second, the Industrial Revolution; an eighteenth of a second, we discover oil; a two-hundredth

of a second, how to split atoms. What we haven't discovered, even now, is how to leave hubris at the door. There's still an overdose of pride in our species. As Voltaire said, "Man learned the art of speech so that his meaning could be hidden."

Once we learned the art of speech, we stopped understanding each other.

AS BIOLOGIST E. O. Wilson of Harvard University points out, we are the first species to grasp the existence of the universe, the biosphere, the whole works. Yet even though we comprehend, we are still doing everything we can to get rid of it. We've picked up some bad habits in the last 500,000 years. As thinking people, as environmentalists, all we have been able to do is to slow down the rate at which things have been getting worse.

I, however, am an optimist. I agree with Pogo, that wise cartoon character from my late middle age, who said, "We have met the enemy and he is us." But I also agree with what Pogo added sometime later: "We are confronted with insurmountable opportunities." In my day, when someone proclaimed a mountain to be insurmountable, it was climbed within a year.

CHAPTER 2

Climbing Mountains

Only the mountain has lived long enough to listen
objectively to the howl of the wolf.

—Aldo Leopold, "Thinking Like a Mountain"

I USED TO BE a mountaineer, and I still enjoy the
company of mountaineers. I never got over my love of climbing, that process by which you and the rock are learning what
you can do with each other.

They credit me with seventy first ascents. Most exhilarating
was the first ascent of Shiprock, on the Navajo Reservation in the
Southwestern United States. Shiprock is tall and jagged, a former
volcanic neck made of rhyolitic breccia that rises 1,500 feet above
the desert floor. From a distance it looks like a windjammer in full
sail. By 1939, when I was twenty-seven, Shiprock had become the
leading challenge to climbers in the United States. Party after
party had attempted its crumbling walls and concluded that the
formation could not be climbed. Bestor Robinson, Raffi Bedayan,

John Dyer, and I were young enough and cocky enough to make another pass at the peak, but with some technological help: expansion bolts, which had never before been used to anchor the belays required in technical mountaineering, and pitons.

We drove our pitons—spikes made of iron or good steel—into cracks that already existed in the rock. If it is the right size crack and the right size piton, it goes in and jams quite well. You've got to have the correct steel so that it can take a little bit of distortion in its shape to accommodate the rock, in order to help make the seal.

Before we drove to the desert, we studied every photograph we could get. We wanted to figure the weaknesses in the mountain's defense. Everybody before us had tried to go all the way up Shiprock's west side. This was understandable, because that was where the only sound rock on the mountain was, a vertical dike of basalt. It's more fun to climb a mountain that's willing to hold itself together, rather than one you have to hold together as you climb it.

From the pictures, we got the idea of proceeding up the dike to the base of the north tower, then fixing a rope and rappelling down a chute, and traversing to the east side and the base of the main tower.

We put the first two expansion bolts to be used in mountaineering at the base of a double overhang, the most challenging pitch of the climb. It's hard to get used to walking on air. Johnny Dyer led it because he was the lightest member of the party, and we could more easily hold him if he fell. Were he not protected by our belays, he could have had a bit of a tumble—about 1,000 feet. Johnny led the two very tough pitches where there was a heavy likelihood of falling, and I led the rest. We wore old-fashioned crepe-soled basketball shoes and exercised a lot of caution. We held group conferences on lofty ledges, spent a restless third night hanging out with the lizards, and finally I was able to yodel victoriously from the narrow topmast that only circling crows had landed on before.

I like to test things. I used to drive a lot of pitons and take them out and look at them to see how well they did. We initiated the use of those expansion bolts. The expansion bolts and pitons made our ascent possible, and they probably saved our lives. Unfortunately, they also damaged the mountain.

THE PROBLEM with all technology, from expansion bolts to nuclear power plants, is that it must be used to correct the errors it invites. Happily, it's easier to take a piton out of a crack than to dismantle a nuclear power plant along the California coast. I have been called a druid often enough, even an archdruid. I don't want to see rampant technology drive the world into going Luddite, destroying technology in the name of preservation; and I still admire scientists, but not when they substitute arrogance for science. I particularly enjoy asking scientists which of their firm beliefs of today they think are most likely to be laughed at in twenty-five years.

I wish that everyone who seeks to lead the environmental cause could experience the peak moments of a climb. There is a lot to be learned from climbing mountains, more than you might think, about life, about saving the Earth, and not a little about how to go about both. Tough mountains build bold leaders, many of whom, in the early days, came down from the mountains to save them. The world now needs these leaders—people willing to take a chance—as it has never needed them before.

John Muir's readers are well aware of his boldness as a mountaineer and wilderness adventurer, whether from his accounts of his ascent of Mount Ritter, his traverse on the narrow ledge under Upper Yosemite Fall, his climb to the top of a storm-tossed tree, or his perils on a glacier in Alaska with his dog Stickeen. Muir was also a bold leader of the Sierra Club. The early leaders of the Sierra Club gained daring from their exploration of Sierra Nevada summits and routes, and seven have had summits named after them. None of them hired guides to lead them. They learned from each other and from the mountains.

What did they learn?

Judgment, for one thing. Climbers with poor judgment can expect to be weeded out early. Whether you climb a mountain for exercise, for challenge, for perspective, "because it's there," or because it's up and you like to keep on top of things, you start out by making judgments.

When you want to get to the top, you need to decide how to avoid the barriers along the way. You take along enough human support and technical protection to give you a chance to fall more than once. You select the best possible route from far enough away so you know where the dead ends are and where you don't want to be if rock or ice decides to fall. You take with you enough training to know your physical limits. You don't expose yourself to more weather than you can handle, and you dress for the worst you can reasonably expect. In the back of your mind you remember that the mountain will be there tomorrow if today it refuses to cooperate. And if your sport is roped climbing, you know that a special kind of love travels both ways along that rope.

You take risks. You search. Sometimes luck is with you, and sometimes not, but the important thing is to take the dare. A new fact has recently become clear to me: It is not variety that is the spice of life. Variety is the meat and potatoes. Risk is the spice of life. Those who climb mountains or raft rivers understand this.

WHAT HAS HAPPENED to boldness in defense of the Earth? For all the splendid increase in membership of the world's environmental organizations, both wilderness and the ecological life-support system of the planet itself are increasingly going down the tubes. Could this be because large environmental groups are acting like government bureaucracies? Consider what my friend Justice William O. Douglas once told President Franklin Delano Roosevelt: Any government bureau more than ten years old should be abolished, because after that it becomes more concerned with its image than with its mission.

In the United States, the environmental movement has saved millions of acres of wilderness, thousands of acres of ancient forests, and rare deserts—saved them for future generations to keep on saving. But for every acre preserved, several have been lost.

Compromise is often necessary, but it ought not to originate with environmental leaders. Our role is to hold fast to what we believe is right, to fight for it, to find allies, and to adduce all possible arguments for our cause. If we cannot find enough vigor in us or our friends to win, then let someone else propose the compromise, which we must then work hard to coax our way. We thus become a nucleus around which activists can build and function.

When the U.S. government proposed dams for the Grand Canyon, we at the Sierra Club said we'd accept no dams. People knew what we stood for and gathered around. We defeated the proposals. If we had said (or thought) that we'd accept one dam but not two, clarity would have vanished from our deeds and faces. People would have seen that we were just arguing about how much defilement is acceptable, not opposing it entirely. They would have gathered elsewhere if they gathered at all. Too often, in the 1990s, environmentalists are so eager to appear reasonable that they have gone soft.

Russell Train, the principal environmental adviser to Richard Nixon, that most contradictory of our "environmental presidents," once said of me, "Thank God for David Brower. He makes it so easy for the rest of us to be reasonable."

I WAS NOT ALWAYS unreasonable, and I am sorry for that. By being just a bit less reasonable, I could have stopped the construction of Glen Canyon Dam, which flooded the last large roadless area between Canada and Mexico, and supplanted it with mechanical recreation areas.

My first victory as executive director of the Sierra Club was helping to stop two dams in Dinosaur National Monument, straddling the Utah-Colorado border. I always like to say, the way to instill youthful confidence and avoid octogenarian burnout is to enjoy at least one consecutive success. We had a few more successes along the way—Point Reyes National Seashore, Fire Island, Cape Cod, Redwood National Park, North Cascades, the national wilderness system—some big wins. I knew what all of these areas looked like. I had been there—rafting the rivers, exploring the canyons, drinking from the springs that cascade out of the high desert walls, some as high as two or three thousand feet. But I had never seen Glen Canyon. I was as blind toward it as my mother, yet, I am sorry to say, without her vision.

I was sitting in the House Gallery, in Washington, D.C., and we had 200 votes to stop the entire Colorado River project. But earlier that day I had received a telegram informing me that the board of our organization had decided to make a compromise. If two dams, Echo Park and Split Mountain, were taken out of the total project, we would withdraw our opposition.

I did not do what a leader should have done, which was hop the next plane to the West Coast and rally the board to righteousness. Instead, I sat on my duff. Now, believe me, the Bureau of Reclamation did not need this dam. It would irrigate nothing. Into the twenty-second century, if then, city dwellers in the region will not need that "placid evaporation tank," as Edward Abbey once described another boondoggle impoundment. Instead, I was uncharacteristically reasonable. I compromised. Now I have to live with that, the flooding of the place no one knew, Glen Canyon.

This is how in 1869 that one-armed explorer, John Wesley Powell, described the canyon none of us will ever see again:

> Past these towering monuments, past these mounded billows of ornate sandstone, past these oak-set glens, past these fern-decked alcoves, past these mural curves, we glide hour after hour, stopping now and then, as our attention is arrested by some new wonder.

I say to all who consider themselves to be the friends of the Earth, and especially to those of you who consider yourselves leaders: Never give up what you haven't seen (unless they be chlorofluorocarbons). And don't expect politicians, even good ones, to do the job for you. Politicians are like weather vanes. Our job is to make the wind blow.

CHAPTER 3

The Bristlecone Pine

Leave it as it is. The ages have been at work on it,
and man can only mar it.

—Theodore Roosevelt

IN NATURE, making the wind blow can be a mistake.
I know, because I tried it.

When I was eleven, I had the idea of raising butterflies. I
liked western swallowtails, which are exquisite creatures, about
three inches in wingspan, yellow with a black border. Just above
the tail they have eye spots of a rainbow hue. My neighborhood
had many swallowtails, and was full of anise—ample butterfly
food. I started with the eggs. Tiny caterpillars emerged, yellow-
banded squibs of black. The caterpillars later turned green and
then into chrysalides. I waited.

When the day came, the first chrysalid cracked. An antenna
popped out. Another. Then the butterfly laboriously climbed
out. The abdomen was extended, full of fluid that was pumped
into the unexpanded wings as the butterfly clung upside down

on a twig. Thirty minutes later, the former caterpillar was aloft. A miracle—which was about to be short-circuited in my desire to help what I did not understand.

As the remaining chrysalides split, I lent a finger. Very gently, I widened their cracking skins. The creatures promptly emerged. They just crawled about. What had been genetically designed had been undone. What was supposed to happen now could not. The flow of fluid was not triggered by the butterflies' own exertions and failed to reach the wings. They all died. I had tried to free them, and by freeing them I had killed them.

WHEN WE WERE fighting to establish a new Redwood National Park, I learned an amazing fact about redwoods. When a 500-year flood deposited deep sediment over the roots, new roots emerged at the right new level, having to punch their way through several inches of bark. Somehow the trees knew how, when, and where to do that. I was freshly impressed with the information that is packed into a redwood seed.

I was also impressed on the roof of a New Yorker's penthouse, seventy stories above asphalt, by a great tree in a small tub producing apples. How does the tree do that? There is a little bit of magic in that tub, and that magic is called soil. To put it teleologically, I like to say: Trees were invented by the soil so it wouldn't have to move.

AS I WAS FOUNDING Friends of the Earth, which is now in fifty-three countries, I suddenly realized that I had never wanted anybody to tell me what to do. I just wanted to coax other people. Respecting the creativity within other people is a hard business to get into.

It occurred to me then that we are like the seeds of the bristlecone pine. Bristlecones grow in the high desert ranges of California and Nevada. On the windward side of White Mountain Peak in California, centuries of wind have stripped their soil away, leaving old roots hanging in the air. The bristlecone pine is the oldest living tree on Earth. The very oldest one we know of was 5,000 years old, and was cut down so a scientist could count the rings.

We don't have to tell the seeds of the bristlecone pine what to do. We give them a chance. Or God does. Or Who It May Concern does. Now, I'm not about to tell a bristlecone pine, or for that matter, a western swallowtail, a condor, or a redwood, what to do. I've learned my lesson well. They know. I am quite willing to ask the rest of us *not* to stop bristlecones from growing. We have no right to drive these miracles off the Earth.

CHAPTER 4

Visions of a Wild Century

> What will it say about the human race if we let the tiger
> go extinct? What can we save? Can we save ourselves?
>
> —Ashok Kumar

LET ME TELL YOU the sad tale of two wild creatures
that you might think have nothing in common: the tiger and
the dolphin. One has fur, the other has fins. One roams the land,
the other the sea. But for both of them, survival is up for grabs.

Outside a shop in Taiwan, a live tiger is staked upside down
inside a cage, legs tethered, head outside the bars. An auction is
going on, and buyers and bystanders alike appraise the imagined
virility of this animal. In the wild tigers may make love several
times an hour, if their mates happen to be in estrus. Some of the
buyers at the shop's auction have flagging libidos, or at least their
customers do, and they all hope that the tiger's vigor will somehow translate to them through the medium of tiger penis soup,
which can cost $320 a bowl. Other customers believe tiger bone
cures rheumatism, or that tiger whiskers impart strength, or that

tiger eye stops certain types of convulsions. The various parts of this dead tiger may bring a retailer as much as $60,000. The auction is soon over. The tiger's throat is slit, and the organs and bone, the penis and pelt, are parceled out to the highest bidders.

Off the coast of Costa Rica, the *Maria Luisa*, a tuna fishing boat, sets its net around a school of disporting dolphins. In the eastern tropical Pacific, the presence of dolphins often indicates yellowfin tuna under the surface. A mechanical winch pulls up the net, and a dolphin is snagged by its dorsal fin and raised high above the ship. The dolphin writhes and twists. The dorsal fin tears off. The net is pulled aboard, as more dolphins are being maimed and drowned. The crew, intent on the tuna catch, rip the mammals from the net. Some are already dead; others still struggle as they are thrown into a chute and dumped overboard as *comida para los tiburones*, "food for the sharks." This day, almost 200 dolphins have been rendered into shark food in the process of catching only twelve yellowfin tuna, a worse than normal ratio. These dolphins happen to be endangered Costa Rican spinners. In the middle of the eastern Pacific, the same story is being played out. The fishermen lay out their huge nets. The noose closes. The tuna are hauled aboard, and with them the dolphins, whose meat few wish to eat. The dolphins are cut from the net, and tossed into the shark chute.

WE KNOW ABOUT the tiger and the dolphin because of the work of biologist Sam LaBudde. Posing as a deckhand on one of those tuna boats, he brought a video camera on board and shot the footage under the guise of making a home movie. He also took pictures of that tiger, and of what happened to it. Decades ago, when our task was to convince people of the need to create national parks and seashores, to preserve wilderness areas, and to save the Grand Canyon, I aimed my 16-millimeter Bell and Howell at Yosemite Valley, at Hetch Hetchy, at a sunset ascent of North Palisade, the highest peak in what was not yet Kings Canyon National Park. When these films were played, people understood what was about to be destroyed, and at their expense. Sam LaBudde knew that eyewitness evidence was still the best.

There are only about 5,000 to 7,500 tigers left in the world, about one-twentieth the number that existed at the turn of the century. Seven to ten million dolphins, including about three-quarters of one species, had been terminated from the eastern Pacific before Sam began to ask the obvious questions: Who is making money from this carnage? How can we let people know what is going on? Should we care?

Sam LaBudde is an intense young man. When he got off the Maria Luisa in 1988, he learned to communicate in six- to eight-second sound bites. He learned to tell people what he had seen in ways that would be effective. But he was still stumped by that third question, Why should we care? He says, "It was like when you walk around in high school or college late at night by yourself or with a friend and try to figure out what truth is, or if there really is a God. I was trying to work out how to make dolphins mean something to all of us. Finally, it occurred to me: Dolphins are the only wild species on the planet that values human life."

When Sam was a machinist in Alaska, people would bring him broken, tortured, and mangled machinery. Sam's job was to make the parts whole again. Every day he learned how to get from Point A to Point B—how to get the job done. He believes that too many environmentalists are process driven these days. As far as being an environmentalist goes, he says, repairing machinery is the most valuable job he could have had. We have to set goals and get the job done.

Sam sits down with a pencil and paper and thinks through the problem: "Tuna sometimes travel with dolphins. Tuna nets kill dolphins. U.S. law allows it (or did). The public does not know the simple truth, that tuna fish sandwiches can cause dolphins to be killed in purse seines. People buy tuna, and essentially pay the fishermen—the tuna canning companies—to go out and kill more dolphins."

In their dolphin campaign, Sam and Earth Island Institute threw up as many roadblocks as they could: emotional, political, legislative, media, consumer, and legal. If they could cut the "circle of destruction" at any point, the whole cycle would stop.

Ultimately, Sam zeroed in on the weakest link in the food chain, which in this case was you and me, and our taste for the little tin cans of tuna sold by H. J. Heinz and other tuna companies. The Heinz people had spent decades creating a wholesome ma-and-pa image for their products, from baby food to dog food. When Sam's video images of what was going on behind the scenes hit the media—and they hit like a freight train—H. J. Heinz realized it could not afford to be characterized as a dolphin-killing company. The stockholders didn't like it much either, and the children of the executives and directors were mostly appalled. The truth about tuna and dolphins even permeated Hollywood. In the movie *Lethal Weapon*, Danny Glover, as a police officer, fixes himself tuna with mayo on white bread. His child stops him: "Dad, don't eat that tuna. You're killing dolphins."

The final blow came when LaBudde organized activists in two dozen major U.S. cities to target Heinz with simultaneous demonstrations a week before the twentieth anniversary of Earth Day. "National Dolphin Day" was to be the day that changed Heinz from a welcome guest in the nation's pantries into "the dolphin-killing company." Instead, Heinz dodged the bullet by convening a press conference in Washington, D.C., forty-eight hours beforehand, and announcing it would no longer buy tuna caught by killing dolphins. Most other U.S. tuna canners quickly followed. National Dolphin Day turned into a celebration.

This was certainly one of the most precipitous changes in consumer buying habits ever to come about, and it all goes back to the pictures, to Sam's courageous use of video. "The visual truth of a situation can move millions of people," he says, "and their outcry moves politicians and bureaucrats. Without visual ammunition we are like unarmed soldiers marching into battle."

Photographs of staked tigers, video of skeletons dumped from bags and reassembled on dirt floors, eerie shots of skinned skulls, and also of fine, finished tiger skins packaged for jaded collectors in the Middle East and elsewhere, all have become the visual ammunition in the battle to save the world's endangered tigers. People have been moved.

But as with dolphins, the causal engine driving the equation is the market, the illegal international trade in tiger parts. It has also played a part in the demise of the African elephant, the rhino, the leopard, scores of beautiful birds such as the scarlet macaw, and even bears from many places in the world. At the turn of the century, the world supported over 1 million rhinos. Now there are fewer than 10,000. Africa and India once had 10 million elephants. Now there are about 600,000.

Incredibly, the illegal trade in bear gall, live birds, leopard skin, rhino horn, tiger bone, ivory, and other wildlife represents the third most lucrative form of international crime, after drugs and gun smuggling. Sam believes the revenue from this macabre commerce is in excess of $2 billion annually. This does not count the cost of interdiction, nor the cost to the economies of the concerned countries. It certainly does not count the cost to the Earth or the tiger. And who would fly to Kenya for a photo safari when the rhinos have been machine-gunned?

ONCE LABUDDE and others around the world put out the visual ammunition concerning the tiger trade, sympathetic governments had the proof they needed to take action against outlaw countries. In 1994 the United Nations-sponsored Convention on International Trade in Endangered Species (CITES) recommended that international trade sanctions be levied against Taiwan for condoning and allowing the commerce. This means that the United

States and other countries that were members of CITES could impose trade sanctions against products coming from Taiwan. That has real economic and political clout. It curbs foul appetites.

The goal of these campaigns is to save the animal. All along, environmentalists must keep asking: How many dolphins have we saved? How many tigers? The amount of money raised, the size of an activist organization, everything else must be subordinated to that question. The Earth demands an honest answer.

Some things must be done now, such as saving the big cats. There is no tomorrow for them unless we insure it today. Other things take time. Restoring habitat, the fragile web that sustains a climax predator such as the tiger, takes a great deal of time. We need to get off our duffs and start now, but we must keep an effort going for fifty, one hundred, even two hundred years, if we wish truly to restore wonders like the tiger habitat, the Everglades in Florida, or the tall grass prairie of the United States, where the buffalo once roamed.

Sam LaBudde says, "You can't promote habitat protection. It's not sexy enough. You've got to use a species as a charismatic symbol. . . . The only international habitat campaign that sells is the rain forest, because it's intriguing. If you shout, 'Save the tall grass prairie!' everybody yawns. They ask, 'What's on the other channel?' Now if you like saving bison . . . "

Of course, Sam is a little young and tough, new school. Well, maybe Sam's right about the need for a "sexy animal" to catch people's interest. But I don't yawn when you say "tall grass prairie." It teaches you what grass roots are all about.

PART II

Solutions

CHAPTER 5

Havens

The greatest beauty is organic wholeness
The divine beauty of the universe . . .
Love that, not man apart . . .

    —Robinson Jeffers

RARE CREATURES such as wolves, grizzlies, buffalo,
trumpeter swans, giant sequoias, and the bristlecone pines still
thrive in the special places we began setting aside for them more
than a century ago. A new kind of foresight brought us Yosemite
and Yellowstone. This was John Muir's legacy, the American
conservation movement. Large blocks of essentially primeval
forest and land were put aside in the Adirondacks of New York,
to be forever wild. Later, some vast reaches of essential habitat
were protected through the Wilderness System.

Unfortunately, too much of what civilization has saved as
wilderness has been called "wilderness on the rocks"—to be
saved, the land was required to be of low commercial value. Too
much was not saved because cities and suburbs crept out from the
edges while their centers decayed.

Thoreau asked long ago, "What's the use of a house if you haven't got a tolerable planet to put it on?" We have been overly enamored of that house and of human beings. We have forgotten the context, without which neither is possible.

Still, we have a fair idea of the beauty that surrounded people a century ago. What do we want the place to look like, and be home to, a century hence?

By setting a goal now, we have a chance to restore what we can of what was needlessly and thoughtlessly lost.

I LIKE THE IDEA of aiming high. Navigators have been aiming at stars for ages. They haven't hit one yet, but they got where they wanted to get because they knew where to aim.

Because our ancestors aimed high, we have sanctuaries that help protect some of our most important species: grizzlies, spotted owls, the marbled murrelet, wolves, and wolverines (the only mammal, Olaus Murie once told me, that doesn't get arthritis). These species are often the best indicators of habitat health. Many biologists call these sanctuaries core reserves. I'd rather call them havens.

All over the Earth there are havens. Some of them even have tigers on them, running free (or as one writer dryly put it years ago, they have wildlife running around uncooked).

The havens are great, but they won't be enough in the long run. Here's what I think we need to do: We need to expand and extend these havens, then surround them with buffer zones that afford somewhat less protection, until we reach the fully developed areas—our cities of the future. These cities would need their own boundaries. Yes, we need boundaries around cities, not around wildness.

Animals and seeds do not honor the straight lines on human maps. They follow river beds, they migrate through mountain passes, they forage from mountain to plain, they pass from public forest to private, they blow where the wind blows. At least they used to.

If members of a particular species find themselves holed up on some island haven, even one as large as Yellowstone Park, for example, they may lose their wanderlust. Havens, even large ones, may not allow for genetic diversity. In addition, in times of stress—when prairies are too hot, or mountains run out of white pine nuts and tasty cutworms, which grizzlies love—then certain animals need to move along to greener pastures. If greener pastures are already occupied, the animals are out of luck.

So to link up these big protected core havens that we already possess to a certain extent in the United States, we would need to add a system of wildlife corridors. I call these corridors, *high ways*, not highways, as in interstates. I like to separate the words "high" and "way" in order to impart some of that original First Nation (or Indian) feeling to the routes that animals and some plants once traveled.

Whatever name you prefer, help it happen. My wife, Anne, and I were fascinated by the creative thinking we encountered in a Wild Earth conference at Sagamore, in the Adirondacks, in 1994. Some thirty-five experts spent three days marking up maps spread out all over the floor, and asking some exciting questions: Where should the cores, buffers, and corridors be between the Atlantic shore and the Great Lakes? Or from the Adirondacks north into the three adjoining provinces of Canada? Conference organizer Dave Foreman's enthusiasm for this kind of planning for the next fifty years was totally contagious. I can't wait to see the composite haven maps published in draft form and the general public asked to answer the question, "What did we forget?"

Plants and animals live in ecosystems, not parks, counties, states, or countries. By protecting havens and linking them with high ways, we would be trying to give fauna and flora what they had before we got here. Creatures live in a community of plants and animals that are recycled by sun, water, and soil.

Let's look at the northern Rockies bioregion as one example: the 18 million-acre Yellowstone ecosystem could be said to be bounded by the Wind, Salt, and Snake rivers to the south, the Yellowstone River to the north, the Clarks Fork to the east, and the valleys of the Gallatin and Madison to the west. In such an ecosystem, all beings, from wolf to lichen, can be seen to be linked. In order to protect the moose, the autotropic bacteria of Mammoth Hot Springs inside Yellowstone Park must also be protected, and with equal determination. The Florida Everglades, the Mojave Desert, and the Amazon are even bigger examples of ecosystems. Of course, an ecosystem can be as small as a rotting deer carcass or as large as the planet itself. Smaller systems are equally fascinating. E. O. Wilson tells us that there are 4,000 to 5,000 species of bacteria in one gram of Norwegian beach-forest soil, and this is glaciated earth. How many species frolic in a gram of soil that glaciers never edited?

LET'S PUT these ideas together: ecosystems, havens, buffer zones, and high ways or corridors.

Take the human-demarcated states of Idaho, Montana, and Wyoming, along with a little swatch of eastern Oregon and Washington, and a chunk of Alberta, in Canada (or let them take us). In this overview Yellowstone Park is a haven. So is Glacier-Waterton International Park. West of Yellowstone is another haven, the Salmon River region, one of the wildest spots in the country, where Marilyn Monroe and Robert Mitchum once filmed *River of No Return*. West of Glacier is a pristine group of forests, mountain ranges, and river valleys that biologists call the Greater Cabinet-Yaak-Selkirk.

On a map these wild areas resemble the four paw prints of a wolf, with the addition of the dewclaw of Greater Hell's Canyon, to the west of the Salmon. If there were high ways running among them, animals would be able to move back and forth in order to replenish their food and sexual stock, when necessary. We would have the beginnings of a restored ecosystem in this part of the northern Rockies.

I have used the northern Rockies as my example, rather than the Adirondacks, or the Southern Appalachians, or northern New England, because I have been quite active in the last couple of years in support of the Northern Rockies Ecosystem Protection Act. (Although the act has many supporters in the United States Congress, virtually none are from those states concerned. This was also the case, unfortunately, in our successful battles in Alaska.) Insiders' determination to exploit was outvoted by outsiders' hope to protect.

I believe that to protect biodiversity, we need to protect big chunks of linked wilderness. You can't do this in just one state, or even state by state. Politically, there is too much risk that the private interests, mining and logging, will chop us apart. They are better organized state by state than they are nationally, compared to environmentalists.

And what of us? We humans are part of the ecosystem, sometimes nicely so, sometimes not. Where, a century hence, might it be most useful for our grandchildren to be?

CHAPTER 6

Cities with Boundaries

What's the use of a house if you haven't got a tolerable
planet to put it on?

—Henry David Thoreau

AS PART of the struggle to save wilderness and Cree
territory in Quebec from Hydro-Quebec, I found myself and
the Cree chief driving into obsolescing northern Manhattan. A
brilliant old idea hit me: Why not give back the beads and offer
him Manhattan?

If New York City had contemplated drawing boundaries
around itself long ago, my idea might have had a chance. But New
York didn't, and my Cree friend had the right answer: "No way."

Cities worked very well, until they lost their main mission,
which was providing a proximity that allowed the gathering and
using of critical human talent and artifacts. Then the winds of
change blew their function away, and we ended up with less
urbia and too much sub. During the Middle Ages in Europe,

47

which I barely remember, cities had walls, models for our going back for the future and bringing it up to date. The peasant farmers of the Middle Ages worked fields outside the city walls. At night, or in times of trouble, they would retreat inside.

Now we've reversed that. Outside our cities lies a ring of suburbs, which have grown over the farms. You can make more money growing condominiums and malls than growing tomatoes. The inside of this un-magic circle, in places like West Oakland, the South Bronx, Albuquerque, or Rocinha, has been abandoned to the poorest people—mostly people of color—who soon become the unlucky ones chosen to receive our gifts of toxic waste dumps and incinerators.

It reminds me of fairy rings. In my decades of traveling on and off Sierra trails, I would come across these common rings of grass. The outside ring, ever expanding, was green and healthy—like new suburbs. Inside the ring—inner city—the grass was dead or dying, the nutrients used up.

Yet cities are essentially good. Without them you'd have to travel forever to find things. A healthy city is a concentration of human creativity, with all the exchanges of ideas and the nurturing of ethics. But they can develop by design, not by default. We've been draining the land around them until there are no farmers, only real estate speculation and, just beyond that, agribusiness. Agribusiness is not interested in farming, that is, in sustaining the soil. Agribusiness mines the soil, and tries its damnedest to addict the soil to chemicals that are disasters to it and, in the long term, to us. And soil, in the long run, is what sustains us.

Once upon a time, there really were cedars in Lebanon, and they existed in profusion. Nepal had more trees. Delhi, in the Central Valley of California, was thirty feet higher, before agribusiness mined the local aquifer, the water table dropped, and its roof collapsed.

In recommending that cities begin to cohere again, with boundaries that make ecological sense, I am not talking about the next few weeks, but the next few decades, the next few centuries.

There can be no slow solutions to fast problems, as Randall Hayes says. Nevertheless, in engineering long-term change, patience is important, lest fear scare off our natural allies. We have a large potential constituency: those who like to eat and breathe well.

Cities with boundaries will have to be creatively designed. We'll have to put a lot of thought into what our rational needs will be in 50 years, or 200 years. This is a fine challenge for architects, builders, engineers, bankers, artists, and all the rest of us. Cities ought not be structured by denial, simply to accommodate whatever the latest failure to think ahead may be. There will be less need for cars and timbered buildings, less junk mail, and less junk TV and the violence it has spawned. Many people have already begun to work at home. Let's encourage this. There really is no reason for suburbs. Cluster these migrant homes, offices, and shops, sometimes in the same building, with orchards on the roof.

Cities are necessary. They can be beautiful. But they need no longer be a plague upon the Earth.

I can't forget what the old city of Dubrovnik was—a World Cultural Heritage site—before the recent madness trashed it. No cars. The marble pavement polished by human feet, no horns sounding, just the almost lost music of friendly human voices.

CHAPTER 7

Eco-Preserves

His signature is the beauty of things.

—Robinson Jeffers

IS IT UNREASONABLE to imagine the Great Barrier
Reef as one glorious, watery Earth Park? Lake Baikal and the
forests of Siberia, a different sort of protected paradise? How
about half of Tibet, the top of the world? The Dalai Lama likes
the idea. It's his.

Shouldn't we all want the top of our world protected?
Shouldn't these places, and more, be set aside, now and forever,
like Yosemite and Yellowstone in the United States? What prevents us from doing so? Ice in our hearts? Blindness to the obvious?

A certain lack of boldness, I think.

It is time to turn on the lights. What is reasonable and what
is not is all a matter of perspective. With the lights on, we can see
that there are a lot of places on Earth worth saving.

One way I turned on the lights was to run full-page newspaper ads.

Way back in January 1969, in a page-and-a-half Sierra Club ad in the *New York Times*, we suggested that the whole Earth should be treated as a conservation district in the universe. The moon, Mars, and Saturn might be nice places to visit, but you wouldn't want to live there (Jupiter, these days, seems especially troubled). We also proposed the idea of treating the planet as a sort of Earth National Park. Our ad raised some eyebrows, paid for itself, and helped get me fired in 1969.

It also helped build support for the World Heritage system, which I consider the most important step in conservation since the national park idea emerged in 1864. The World Heritage idea was initiated a century later, in the 1960s, by Judge Russell Train, then president of The Conservation Foundation.

I watched his idea take place, supported by that January ad and by books from the Sierra Club and Friends of the Earth. In 1972 it was ratified by the United Nations. Since then, more than one hundred nations have approved more than four hundred areas of outstanding natural or cultural importance. Most of these places—such as Yosemite or Redwood national parks, the Grand Canyon, or the Parthenon—already had some kind of protection.

A group of us working with Russ came up with one hundred unprotected and endangered areas that to this day remain on a waiting list. The nations containing them have not yet seen fit to nominate them. World Heritage is a bold concept, one not yet completed.

THE GALÁPAGOS ISLANDS, of Ecuador, are in the World Heritage, thanks to many organizations and individuals, including Loren Eiseley, Russ Train, ecologist John Milton, and Eliot Porter, the photographer whose two great exhibit-format books on the islands, edited by Kenneth Brower, helped save Galápagos wildlife from eradication by colonialization. The islands were a big revelation for everybody, starting with Charles Darwin, who could be said to be the founder of modern ecology. Journeying to the Galápagos on the HMS *Beagle*, Darwin discovered that all life on the planet, from people to plankton, was part of a complex blanket spread over the globe. There can be no pulling of one thread in that blanket, without nubbing the weave, or worse, unraveling the fabric.

So I was glad to visit the Galápagos, at long last, once I finally got there on my way to the Earth Summit in Rio de Janeiro in 1992.

Our eldest son, Kenneth, visited the Galápagos twenty-five years before I did, and stayed three months. Among the many people he interviewed was Miguel Castro, the conservation officer of Darwin Station. Miguel's description of how tortoises die (an old tortoise may be 200) was interpreted by Ken in the Sierra Club volumes *Galápagos: The Flow of Wildness*: Once he gets big, a tortoise has no enemies, and if he avoids falling over a cliff or into a lava pit too steep for escape, he dies only of old age. One day he gets too weak to move, and stops. He stays in that spot for months, sometimes, his long practiced power of enduring, his racial skill at it, serving him long after his power to move and get food has failed. 'Watching leaves fall, probably, and the seasons change. . . . The tortoise living only in his head and eyes . . . a spark still somewhere inside, above the plastron and below the dome.

SIBERIA LIES FAR across the Pacific from the islands of the Galápagos, but the forests of Siberia circumscribe another of the jewels of the Earth: Lake Baikal. Lake Baikal is the oldest, deepest lake on the planet. It holds one-fifth of the world's liquid fresh water. Another fifth is held by our own Great Lakes, and another fifth by the waters of the Amazon. Baikal used to be three miles deep, but that was 25 million years ago. Sedimentation has filled in two miles of its depth. In short, it is still a deep lake.

In California and Nevada, our biggest lake is Tahoe. Tahoe would fit in a blustery cove of Baikal. Were it to be plopped down in our part of the world, Baikal would run from San Francisco to Tijuana—the length of California's Central Valley.

Lake Baikal is home to some 1,800 species that do not exist elsewhere. It is a treasure house of living treasures. Baikal holds the world's only landlocked freshwater seals, the nerpa, which are still hunted to get fur for hats. Of course, we (and the old Russians) hunted otters off Northern California long ago, and harp seals in northern Canada not so long ago, but today we know that this is a dumb idea.

Beauty has become as big an industry as lumbering, even mining, and certainly fur trading. Tourism has been estimated to be a trillion-dollar business on this planet, and eco-tourism is its cutting edge (although I would like to see the tour organizers remember to share the revenue fairly with the countries being toured). The Russians may miss the windfall if the nerpa are kept too nervous to be a tourist attraction. Killing exotic freshwater seals for fur has the same effect on tourism as machine-gunning elephants in Kenya for the ivory, or selling a lion hide for $1,000, while that lion, kept alive, could produce $500,000 in tourist revenue.

If cattle ranches in Australia are being turned into bird-watching sanctuaries, I hope the Russians will realize that one live nerpa willing to show off is worth a hundred that have been butchered.

ECOLOGICAL PRESERVES are not easy to create. Indigenous peoples are not eager to leave home just to please tourists (nor should they be forced to). It is generally a long, cool day before the individual country will nominate such a preserve. They have the same problem with developers we have. Developers have their own ideas about what to do with a resource such as Lake Baikal, the Grand Canyon, Mineral King, Mount Everest, or Hilton Head. They want to use it up. We just want it to last.

But why limit our thinking?

I'm now looking for help in turning on more lights in behalf of ecosphere reserves—the ecosphere being that part of the Earth that is life giving. We in the United States, brief tenants that we are, have an obligation to set a global example in truly wise use of land. We can respect the freedom of unnumbered future tenants. I like the goal of George Dyson, a bright young designer of seagoing canoes: "to find freedom without taking it from someone else." How many of the freedoms that we enjoy have been taken from other cultures?

To begin with, we can expand the Biosphere Reserve concept initiated by the U.N.'s "Man in the Biosphere Program." We can establish in the United States a National Ecoreserve System (NES). We now have reserves but no system. It took us fifty-two years from the first national park (Yosemite) to establish the National Park System in 1916, giving parks the protective clout they needed.

We can give our present biosphere reserves some recognition and clout by putting them in the NES. Add inadequately protected lands, federal, state, local, and provate. Devise incentives to encourage private owners to help out. Establish performance standards—criteria for managing the land—to protect its biodiversity and provide some public access. Great Britain does this with its national parks, some privately owned. Wonderful signs guard the areas: "Please close the gate behind you" and "Be tidy." There's even one that says: "It is forbidden to cast stones at this notice. By order of the Surrey County Council."

To help this happen, change the name and mission of the Bureau of Land Management to the National Land Service (NLS). Give it a role in protecting all U.S. land, not just public land. Put the NES in the NLS. Easy to say. Hard to do. Essential to sustainability.

How about the rest of the world? How to get those areas on the waiting list of the World Heritage finally protected? How to go beyond World Heritage to protect areas of the Earth currently endangered, such as the forests of Siberia or the Amazon?

One way, and a good way to pay for this goal, would be to establish a World Ecological Bank (WEB), which would be as devoted to conserving, preserving, and restoring the Earth's ecological capital as the present-day World Bank is to expending it. WEB is a great acronym because it reminds us of the "webness" of life.

Through the WEB, nations could nominate areas of outstanding natural or cultural significance that reside in *other* nations. But through the WEB they would pay for the privilege. This would make it fair (or more fair) to the countries holding the designated areas, because it would defray the costs, and compensate those countries for the loss of old-fashioned extractive uses—logging, mining, and the rest—until alternative economic uses were developed for the areas as reserves that transcend national boundaries (economic uses that did not trash them), or until the host countries had the money to designate these areas as national parks.

By this process, interested WEB nations could nominate a substantial part of Tibet, for instance, as an international Peace Park. This is what the Dalai Lama has suggested. Until the Free Tibet effort succeeds, China could be paid to stop draining Tibet's natural capital.

Taiwan might be a nation willing to help pay to see Tibet's natural capital and great beauty spared, and we in the United States, Great Britain, or Germany might help pay Taiwan to change its appetite for tiger parts. Everybody should be willing to pay for the tiger nations, such as India, to protect their tigers.

In a sense, this is a global form of reverse colonialism. Parts of Canada and Southeast Asia could use some of the same help. Maybe even our own Pacific Northwest. Russia, certainly, could be paid to prohibit the clearcutting of Siberia's forests.

It is easy to be an alarmist if you comprehend what the vultures hovering over the pieces of the old Soviet Union are up to. They are trying to take everything they can get, chumming the Russians with hard cash. Actually, they are giving vultures a bad name. The oil companies want the oil. There's lots, and I'm not against our using oil, but I am against the rate at which we are exhausting it, be that in Alaska or Russia. The forest companies, such as Japan's Mitsubishi, are eyeing Siberia as if it were the new Amazon. To them it is. It should be to us, too, for different reasons.

The rain forests of Brazil, and forests of the rest of the Earth, are the lungs of the planet, putting out oxygen and locking up carbon. A quarter of the world's remaining forests are in Siberia. Those of us who are hooked on oxygen should be willing to pay Siberia to keep exporting oxygen instead of liquidating its forests.

I wish I were twenty years younger to work on this one.

I'd like to see if WEB could find a way to subsidize the maintenance of those magnificent Siberian forests. Ecologically sound selective cutting would help their economy without destroying yet another place most of us have not yet seen. (I can't forget Glen Canyon.) Nature, in trying to provide a surplus of everything, has let our numbers and also our appetites overdraw from that surplus. Without that overdraft, the trees in Siberia would be all right.

Another way to pay for "webness" would be to have every foundation in the world invest 10 percent of its equity in a revolving fund that would provide major financial backing to the new World Ecological Bank. This would be taking global the national example of the Nature Conservancy. It would allow foundations to make history.

The political power of foundation board members would strengthen the ability of respective governments to acquire and protect outstanding ecoreserves. The foundation investment could be recovered and reused. It could even be used to buy out exploiters. Let generous individuals—and governments—add to this World Ecological Fund of the World Ecological Bank.

I think a man like Russ Train, whom I consider the most outstanding Republican conservationist, should be put in charge of this Big Idea.

What we need in these perilous times is a consummate negotiator between the Earth and its human predators.

Let us now resolve to give the Earth the care we give— and this may surprise you—Yosemite. I've been going there for seventy-six years, and during that time the number of annual visitors grew from 37,000 to 4 million. Despite all those people, it looks better now than it did in 1918 or in the mid-thirties, when I worked there. I know of no other famous place that has pleased so many people and suffered so little impact.

I tell people who don't like the crowds in Yosemite Valley that I can take them in ten minutes to a place where they won't see anybody else all day. Unfortunately, the Park Service wants to build a parking lot there for 1,800 cars. Let's not let them! I'd rather see the old Yosemite Valley Railroad restored and electrified and the cars parked in Merced. Cover the cost with sin taxes (and I'll pay my share gladly).

That's a better way to treat the world's first eco-preserve—if you don't count Eden.

CHAPTER 8

Forest Revolution

If today is a typical day on planet Earth, we will lose
116 square miles of rain forest . . .

—David W. Orr, environmental scientist

EVER SINCE the cedars of Lebanon started going down
to the sea in ships, we have failed to remember that photosyn-
thesis makes it possible for creatures like us to breathe. The forest
and forest soil are the essential elements of the Earth's thin, dy-
namic, beautiful skin.

All over the world, we are running out of old growth trees—
our redwoods, Douglas firs and mahogany, pines and ipe, Sitka
spruce and teak, cedar and monkey puzzle. For a long time, paper
has been made from softwoods, such as fir and pine, but recent
technological advances allow giant timber corporations to pulp
hardwoods as well. The chain saws are being turned on mature
oaks in Mexico's Sierra Madre, soft maples in New England,
alders, poplars, and aspens, as well as countless tropical trees that
were once well off limits. Even cottonwoods, the gnarly giants

of rivers and riparian zones in the American West, are being ripped for cheap coffins. No tree is safe. The information society demands more, not less, paper for printers, copiers, and fax machines. Developing countries are converting their tropical hardwoods into textbooks. Democracy means more newsprint, and higher literacy calls for more books.

Simply put, what's left of the world's old growth forests is being savaged for two overweening purposes: building materials and paper pulp. A quarter of the trees cut down on the planet each year go to timber for two-by-fours, beams, plywood flooring, and the rest; while another eighth are killed to provide paper. There is also a horrendous desire for packaging materials, and in developing countries, a tremendous current demand for cooking fuel.

Everybody knows this. But what most people don't know is that it no longer has to be or can be this way.

We are on the verge of a forest revolution. It is not necessary to make paper from trees. It is no longer necessary that so many houses and buildings be constructed from wood and forest products, at least not in the way we have become accustomed to in the United States, Canada, Japan, and Scandinavia. It is no longer necessary to use so much wood for cooking and heating. How do we change the way things are, to the way they ought to be? I have some ideas.

LET'S TAKE the easy one first: cooking fuel. One-half of the world's trees cut every year are cut for cooking fuel. Charcoal is just a lighter energy-intensive form of fuel wood, and it takes twice the energy to burn wood down to charcoal.

The long-term solution—and we need to expedite this right away—is solar cookers. These are tailor-made for the bare-necessity fuel users of the world, and there are billions of them. They have to eat, and if it's starch they have to cook it.

For the time being, however, natural gas is probably the most practical alternative, especially in the huge urban areas of the world's South. Nigeria and Mexico, for example, are major pro-ducers of natural gas, or could be. Two-thirds of the world's nat-ural gas production is still burned off, or flared, at the wellhead. With the price of oil flat these days, the oil industry should wel-come the opportunity to make out on gas and save forests in the process.

NOW THAT WE'RE warmed up, let's tackle some other problems that are chewing up our forests: papermaking and building mate-rials. The obvious solution is to substitute other things for wood in the making of paper and in the construction of houses and commercial structures.

First, some good news. One of the largest builders of private homes in the United States, the Del Webb Corporation, has begun to replace wooden two-by-fours—the bone and sinew of modern architecture—with steel stud framing. There are some minor problems. It can be tricky, for example, to hang wallboard and sheetrock from steel, but pneumatic staplers have been invented that can puncture metal as well as wood. In the early 1990s Del

Webb built about 100,000 new homes using steel instead of wood. The steel industry likes this development. Larger boards and beams are being fashioned from laminated wood, or engineered wood, as it is called, which is put together from smaller pieces using new glues, new processes—but beware of carcinogenic glues. This allows us to do something with all the pieces that would go to waste after the large boards have been cut.

The timber industry is also becoming more efficient. Technology has made it possible to take a look inside a tree, and then direct the cut with a computer, in order to eliminate waste and maximize the number of usable beams and two-by-fours. In the past, 40 percent or more of a felled log was considered unsuitable for lumber.

Some uses for lumber are even more wasteful. About 11,000 acres of Ohio forest are cut each year to make pallets, the wooden skids used everywhere—and tossed—in modern trucking and warehousing. Pallets can be made just as easily from plastic, and are beginning to be. In Europe pallets are recycled, like beverage bottles, and come with a returnable deposit.

Recycling wood is an idea for the coming decade, as Peter Warshall points out. Scrap wood clogs our landfills, but most of it can be recovered. Old pallets can be pulped. Houses can be dismantled by hand instead of by bulldozer. It's a labor-intensive process that could reduce homelessness. The wood can be reused instead of buried in landfill. Reuse will keep the wood's carbon locked up. This is not pie in the sky. It will be a whole new industry, much like the recycling of aluminum cans and glass bottles.

Already many builders separate scrap wood when they are building and demolishing houses. Soon, landfill operators will be paying for that old lumber instead of charging to accept it— especially old barn siding that has been beautifully weathered.

Here's a challenge for the timber giant Weyerhaeuser, among others: For every 100 pounds of recyclable paper an environmentally concerned family turns in, will you guarantee to preserve as much primeval forest? For every 1,000 board feet of demolition lumber a green carpenter or construction company loads into your bins, will you agree to turn over as much ancient forest as it takes to make that amount of paper, or lumber, to, say, the Nature Conservancy? With the help of Justice Douglas, I got the Nature Conservancy its first $6 million line of credit. I like them.

What we need to do is to tie conservation directly to the preservation of old growth—a term subject to too many unhelpful interpretations. I prefer "primeval" or "ancient forest." I'm old growth myself, and that's not nearly old enough—or diverse enough. Biodiversity, varying beautifully from region to region, is what forests are all about.

My plan could have regional charm, in the United States, Europe, or anywhere. Caring people everywhere would know what biodiversity they were saving in their own bioregion. I believe this challenge would work, and we should try it.

Some of us—especially Americans, Canadians, Scandinavians, and the Japanese—are wood-lovers. This is not necessarily the case in hot, humid countries like the Philippines and Brazil, where the houses of wealthy people are often made of stone and cement, since wooden houses are subject to termites and other insects. In many tropical countries, it is the poor people who use cheap wood. We must encourage them to build from reinforced stone and adobe. Beautiful beams, redwood, teak, and mahogany, are still the high-end components of the gourmet housing industry. Here, perhaps, a cultural change is in order.

This wood is beautiful, but so is a polar bear rug or a sealskin hat. Many thoughtful consumers would not decorate their hearths with newly killed bear skin or wear real leopard. In the coming years, they may ask themselves if using giant redwood and mahogany is really such a good idea. They may decide, also, not to order from a mesquite grill, as they learn that old growth mesquite in Mexico and the American Southwest is being extinguished for mere human fashion—like beaver, like nerpa, like tiger.

I put redwood siding on our own house in 1946. I love it, but I would not use redwood again.

THE WORDS you are reading right now have not been printed on paper pulped from any tree. I write upon flowers, as it were. The paper in *Let the Mountains Talk* has been manufactured from kenaf, which is a twelve-foot cousin of cotton and okra, a variety of flowering hibiscus, *Hibiscus cannabinus*. Kenaf is a tough, fibrous annual, far richer in cellulose—which is what paper is made from—than are pine and wood. (Note: This edition is printed not on kenaf but on 100 percent recycled paper containing at least 50 percent post-consumer waste.)

The story of kenaf is interesting. In 1916 the United States government predicted the country could run out of trees by the end of the century. It was a prescient bit of forgotten science, that study. At the beginning of World War II, the U.S. Navy also did some hard thinking. Rope, once used rather a lot by sailors, was made from jute and hemp. It came mostly from the Philippines, which our then-opponents, the Japanese, controlled. The U.S. Department of Agriculture was asked to come up with some sub-stitutes. They did a couple of studies, involving hundreds of plants. By process of elimination—what could be easily farmed? what made the best rope or paper?—kenaf, with hemp, came to the top of the list. And because of its longer fiber, kenaf may be recycled more easily than paper from wood pulp.

Some other people were not so hot on the idea. Dupont natu-rally preferred nylon for making rope, since they had invented it. They lobbied hard. (When you've been around awhile, you notice certain similarities. Dupont makes its money from nylon, from chemicals, not from farm products like kenaf. The automo-bile and tire companies make their profits from cars, and the oil companies from gas and oil. Standard Oil, General Motors, and Firestone lobbied successfully to rip out the municipal train tracks in Los Angeles and in some other American cities. No money was to be had from rail transportation, at least for them.) At any rate, Dupont won the rope wars. It did not hurt the argument that hemp was smoked by jazz musicians and African-Americans.

Kenaf did not carry hemp's psychoactive baggage, but after the war, further substitutes were no longer needed. There was nylon for rope. For paper, there were the glorious coastal temperate rain forests of Northern California, through Oregon, Washington, British Columbia, and right on to the Tongass forest in Alaska.

In the 1970s, when newsprint prices spiked a bit, those old kenaf studies were pulled off the shelf. The U.S. government paid to test some Illinois-grown kenaf between the rollers of the *Peoria Times*. It worked, but then newsprint prices dropped. There was still cheap pulp to be had from trees, and kenaf was again forgotten.

In the 1980s the big paper companies continued to marry the big lumber companies, and with so much go-go junk bond money around, they built very large mills, like nothing seen before on Earth. One of these supermills processes 400,000 tons of pulp a year. In the 1960s there were only one or two of these monsters. Now there are some fifty. In the 1960s there were more than 100 so-called mini-mills. Now there are only about thirty.

Is this good for anybody? Is it good for the Earth? Profits are now pitiful in the paper industry. Americans are out of work in the paper industry. The behemoths have severe overcapacity, and they are sucking up the forests of the planet to feed the maw. Anything is grist for the mill, and the scientists, instead of thinking up substitutes, are designing shredders and chemicals that can pulp any tree still living.

It is instructive to know that those countries, like China, which killed their trees and settled their wilderness long ago, no longer use trees for paper. They cannot. They have been forced to find substitutes, from rice to kenaf. I like to read. I like forests on the sides of my mountains. There is still a choice, for many countries.

Right now it costs more to make paper from kenaf than from cheap, heavily subsidized wood pulp. This is essentially a problem of start-up and of scale. More kenaf needs to be grown, and initially given a fraction of the subsidy wood gets. Smaller mills need to be built near kenaf farmlands. This will happen when the market is expanded. There was no market for recycled paper—what a strange idea—when I returned from World War II. Now thousands of companies do business on recycled paper. Recycled paper makes money, and it saves trees. In fact, if we could expand our use to about 40 percent, we would save an enormous amount of primeval forest.

By the way, it is important to realize that much of what passes for "recycled" is often no more than a byproduct of paper-making—the punched holes in notebooks, for instance, or envelope trimmings. True recycled paper is paper that has been used, recovered, repulped, and made into usable paper once more.

To create the market for tree substitutes, I would like to see the San Francisco and New York phone books printed on kenaf. How could that come about? Let's be bold. A lot of environmentalists live in those cities. Over 300,000 members of Greenpeace, alone, live in California, and there are some 1.7 million in the United States. There are 12 to 15 million dues-paying members of environmental organizations in the United States. That is a lot of requests for tree-free phone books, or, for that matter, bond stationery and book-quality printing paper. At the moment, kenaf is a high-end product. Stationery, cards, and books printed on kenaf already make good sense.

The federal government recently mandated that a certain percentage of its paper be printed on recycled wood fiber. Its departments should start using tree substitutes, like kenaf, in the same way, and also cotton and corn husks. The Italians and the Japanese are already doing it. The Germans are now the leaders in the multibillion dollar pollution-control industry. Must so much of American industry continually primp and posture as Detroit did thirty years ago, when its automakers scoffed at the visions of Volkswagen and Toyota?

Why does this happen? Because the timber and paper companies in this country (and the world) are far more heavily subsidized by their governments than the public suspects. They comprise a very powerful planetary country club. Taxpayers and consumers everywhere are being bled by the lumber barons of Japan, Canada, New York, and Houston because true costing, not to mention the cost to the Earth, is not invoked by industry economists. No wonder economist and futurist Hazel Henderson calls economics a form of brain damage.

It is a hidden subsidy to big timber for the taxpayer to pay the Forest Service for building roads into the best virgin forests. It is a hidden subsidy that these companies can come onto public land, clearcut the forests, and not even have to plant more. Or, if they plant more, to brag about the number of trees but forget to mention they are replacing an insignificant fraction of the volume they have removed. It will then be necessary for taxpayers, for generations to come, to cover the cost of replacing the excellence of, say, a 500-year-old tree and its surroundings. This is an enormous subsidy. When you add the cost to you of all these subsidies, you are probably paying far more—on April 15th of every year—for a book printed on wood pulp than for one printed on unsubsidized kenaf.

Will timber people once again, as they did under the Weeks Act in 1911, sell their derelict land at a profit to the government, which must pay (and charge taxpayers for) the restoration bill? Clearcutting and quick lumbering cause erosion. Erosion removes soil. Soil is what grows trees. That's a loss to future farmers. It is also a loss to pharmaceutical companies. So many drugs, from digitalis to quinine to yew-based cancer amelioratives, have been synthesized from forest plants, from primeval stands that are disappearing fast, as fast as one football field a second, in the tropical rain forests.

Politics can both cause the damage and require the cure. Why should the timber industry be allowed to kill the fishing industries of the United States, Canada, Mexico, Indonesia, the Philippines, and any other *terra firma* they chance to touch? Along with dams, the reason we don't have many salmon on the West Coast is largely because streams have been silted by clearcuts, which export soil and muddy the spawning beds.

At the moment, the governments of the world, certainly ours, value a tree only after it is cut down. But a tree has other responsibilities. Ask a bald eagle what the worth of a tree is. Ask a grizzly, who cannot prosper near roads cut into the forest. Ask the soil. Unless soil happens to be in a traveling mood, it values tree roots very highly. Especially after heavy rain.

And all over the Earth, even in our man-made deserts, a hard rain is beginning to fall.

Some of this rain is laced with acid from our factories. Using substitutes for lumber and for timber-pulp paper saves forests. Recycling saves forests. But in the northeastern United States, in eastern Canada, in Europe, acid rain is killing the trees before environmentalists and timber companies have a chance even to do battle over the end product. If we had less acid rain, we would have more forests.

There is a terrible word, in Germany, for what is going on. It is *waldsterben*: "forest death."

The Germans have gone as far as any of us in their attitude toward protecting forests. In Germany it is seen as a privilege to have trees on your property. In America, where some 73 percent of the forests are on private, not federal, lands you can do pretty much what you want with your trees. Not so in Germany. Germany issues tree licenses, much like driver's licenses. This would be pretty hard to swallow for many Americans, those that own trees, at least until they face their own death. Then the German system has its advantages. In America valuable trees are counted as assets. When an owner dies, the heirs must pay inheritance taxes on their value. This hurts, especially in the American South. To soften taxes in the United States, owners of beautiful forests cut them when they feel a certain chill. Or their children cut them soon after the funeral. This is stupid. It hurts the Earth.

Germany has tax incentives to maintain private forests, and we should have them, too.

If, in America, mortgage rates go up, housing starts go down. The price for timber falls. Suddenly, substitutes make less sense, outside the committed. When the dollar drops, that's worse. Then American timber is sold to Japan for a song. The Japanese are smarter than we are. They bury our old growth under water. They take the best logs from the Pacific Northwest, worth millions, and save them in the cold, preserving brine of their seas. To them, wood is gold. The price can only go up.

WE ARE ENTERING a twenty-year period that can either spell the end of beautiful trees as we know them, or that can save them. Here I want to stop and make some distinctions. What is really at stake right now is the primeval forest Longfellow admired in *Evangeline*. These are, usually, the closed canopy forests, perhaps the cathedral redwoods, where some of the trees tower 100 meters into the sky, or the Sitka spruce groves of British Columbia, or what is still virgin in the Amazon. What is no longer at stake are the gang-raped tropical rain forests of Papua New Guinea, Indonesia, and Malaysia. There will never be places like this on Earth again. We can save what's left. It is like saving the Grand Canyon. It must be done if enough of the pages of the poem that is the Earth are to remain whole.

Since 1600 the United States has lost 95 percent of its ancient forests. This does not mean that we don't have tremendous forests. The difference has been made up by secondary growth. In fact, in many states we are putting back in numbers as much as we are taking off. But in volume or in quality, we aren't even coming close. It is not the original good stuff, and of course it cannot be. Primeval forests represent the treasure troves of biodiversity and time. That is what makes them irreplaceable. You will never see again what we cut now; you will see nothing like it or the non-human community it nurtures.

IT IS NOT too late to practice sustainable eco-forestry. The mammoth monoculture tree plantations of Chile, New Zealand, and elsewhere are on the wrong track. This is crop farming, with Monterey pine as the soybean. But the vulnerability of monoculture has escaped the forestry schools, industry, and the Forest Service throughout this century. We need to use the product conservatively and grow forest diversity—not single-species plantations on the assumption that the Second Coming will spare us from tomorrow. We can reform. Public interest and private forestry can make sense, and need to.

There have been good timber companies and I have known good timber executives, such as Ike Livermore, a friend of mine and of wilderness for sixty years. I often disagreed with Ike, but never with rancor. When he was secretary of the Pacific Lumber Company, Ike liked to hear redwoods fall. But he didn't want too many redwoods to fall too soon, the way the takeover artists from Maxxam do. They acquired Ike's company in a hostile takeover in 1986, and are drastically overcutting to pay off their junk bonds and move on. Ike didn't advocate a thousand-year cutting cycle, which I think would be about right for redwoods, but his Pacific Lumber Company came closer to it than any other outfit in the board-foot crowd. And if you were a logger for Pacific Lumber, before it was chainsawed by Maxxam, you got about the highest wages in the industry, and even an $8,000 college scholarship for your kid.

I remember a conversation I once had with Pete Seeger, the great folksinger and champion of cleaning up the Hudson River. He said, "If you don't walk along with someone as far as possible, there can be no conversation." So walk with people you do not agree with, gathering their point of view. Put yourself in their shoes, prepared to learn and to persuade. If that doesn't work, it's time for full-page ads, time to marshal the troops, by the millions if you've got them. They are there, because everybody breathes and our very atmosphere is at risk. There is only one Earth.

The environmentalists of the world must not be so naive as to think they have won if they stop Maxxam, Mitsubishi, the timber princes of Djakarta, or Burger King from killing ancient forest stands from British Columbia to Costa Rica to Montana to the Penang Peninsula. Rust never sleeps. There is a timber industry term called *coyoting*. If logging isn't profitable on one forest, trot over the ridge to the next. Douglas fir in Canada makes terrific pulp. Canada's environmentalists raise a hue and cry? Maybe Mexican tree-huggers are not yet so well organized. Pulp is pulp and old growth oak on the Sierra Madre squishes just as well.

We who would defend the Earth must look in the mirror. We are endangered. Time is running out. If a small child wields a kitchen knife, you do not try to wrestle it away. You offer a substitute—a toy, a cookie, anything. If we want a future by design, not default, it's time for a rebirth of creativity. History tells us all too clearly what it costs to run out of forests. Man has created deserts with great skill in the past, and is speeding the process today.

By buying this book, printed on kenaf, you contribute toward the rescue of forests in Siberia, Canada, the United States, and everywhere else. My publisher paid a little more for this paper, but we all get paid back in the long run, by the taxes you and coming generations will not have to pay to subsidize the unnecessary pulping of forests.

You are helping build the demand that will encourage others to meet it. And there is further reward in your knowing that the unpulped trees can keep a lot of forest beautiful in perpetuity. That kind of perpetuity brought the forests from prehistory to you. Let it remain the essential element in what Wallace Stegner, one of the most creative of writers, called the Geography of Hope.

CHAPTER 9

More Monks

Trend is not destiny.

—René Dubos

ASKED HOW MANY people the Earth can sustain indef-
initely, Harvard professor E. O. Wilson, certainly one of the
world's great biologists, replied: "If they have the appetite for
resources of Japan and the United States, 200 million." This was
reported to me in Kyoto by Dr. David Suzuki, Canadian biologist
and commentator. I'd never heard so low a figure, and finally got
Professor Wilson on the telephone to check up. Had he said that?
"No," he responded, "but it sounds reasonable."

He gave me some people to refer to further, including population researcher and author Anne Ehrlich. She gave me an esti-
mate at the 1991 Land, Air, and Water Conference, in Eugene,
Oregon: "With a little more industrial development in the Third
World, 500 million."

In other words, the Earth is now supporting (but not very well) ten times more people than it can handle over the long run. We are surviving by severely overdrawing life's account in the World Resource Bank. OK so far, as the man said after falling forty stories with only ten to go.

Somewhere I picked up a staggering statistic: In the past twenty years the United States has used up more resources than all the rest of the world in all previous history. I haven't checked that figure. I like it the way it is. If it isn't right yet, we seem determined to make it right. Wrong.

"Trend is not destiny," the late René Dubos wrote. I do not blindly oppose progress. I oppose blind progress. We had better not let the U.S. trend become the Earth's destiny. We don't need to.

I don't know about life after death, but I do believe in life after birth. And it is absolutely essential that we take steps to make that life after birth a better one. Here are some key steps to take. Try hard not to be offended by them:

First, improve the literacy of women and leave the number of children to be born up to them—the nurturers, not the passersby.

Second, improve nutrition and medical care and thus reduce the number of children thought necessary for survival of our species.

Third, improve all other forms of social security for the same reason. Remember James Reston's admonition when he was a New York Times editor: "We have no more right to tell a man how many children he may have than how many wives he may have."

I found myself unable to stop telling this admonition in time when addressing an audience in Utah, and escaped by pointing out that the number of children is a social problem, and the number of wives merely an organizational problem.

Perhaps someone should take the Pope to lunch and explain things to him. Perhaps the Dalai Lama should. He told a Berkeley audience on a sunny day in 1994: "The solution to the population problem is—more monks!"

CHAPTER 10

Hypercars

Ready or not, we're all about to embark on one of the
greatest adventures in industrial history.

> —Amory Lovins

I WAS LISTENING to Amory Lovins last year. Amory
was saying: "The biggest change in industrial structure since
the microchip will be a revolution in what cars are, how they're
made, how they're sold, and even how they're driven. I call these
vehicles—*hypercars*."

When Amory talks, I am careful to listen. He is usually right
as rain—rain before we added acid. I also like a modest beginning:
"the biggest change in industrial structure since the microchip."
And I know that if hypercars come on-line soon, environmentalists, like everyone else, will have some retooling to do. Or it will
be a wilder century than we all might like to think.

Amory Lovins was once a don at Merton College, Oxford
University, and I think he was the youngest fellow to hold that

position in 400 years. He was shaking things up at Harvard when he was sixteen. He completed his undergraduate experience long before reaching the drinking age—which he has declined to exploit. I've never persuaded him to take a drink. Sometimes I think that one of my greatest achievements was persuading Amory Lovins to give up being a don. He was in physics then. Just soon enough, he invented the soft energy path.

After he returned to the United States, Amory wrote a paper for Bill Bundy at *Foreign Affairs* called "Energy Strategy: The Road Not Taken," which was the most popular article *Foreign Affairs* ever published.

Amory challenged everything. He said America had too much energy, that the hydro-nuclear-coal-electric grid was silly, often unnecessary, heavily subsidized by the taxpayers, dangerous, and uneconomic, that the peaceful atom was a myth masking a bloated war machine, and why bother, anyhow? This shook some of us, but Amory had the figures to back himself up. He always does. Then he suggested some ways out of the jungle: solar and efficiency. Amory cofounded the Rocky Mountain Institute near Aspen. He designed its stone and wood building's energy systems so that even at 40 degrees below zero, it is 99 percent solar-heated.

Some people have scoffed at Amory, because, quiet as he is, he rocks their boat. But some people have changed their lives according to Amory's predictions; others have unscoffed all the way to the bank. So when Amory began to talk of hypercars, I was prepared to listen, and I hope you are, too. I turn this chapter over to the capable hands of Amory Lovins.

The hypercar represents a leapfrog in the art of designing and building cars. The hypercar artfully fuses together the best available technology for ultralight construction and hybrid-electric drive. I want to emphasize the synergy between these two technologies. People have made ultralight cars. They weigh two to four times less than normal cars, and they're about two or two-and-a-half times more efficient. People have also made hybrid-electric cars, but if you put hybrid drive in a heavy car, it only improves efficiency by about 30 percent to 50 percent. If you put ultralight and hybrid together in the same car, which has really not been done yet, but could be, then you're getting a factor of five to twenty gain in efficiency. It's one of those "1 + 2 = 10" equations.

Hypercars will be able to drive from New York to Los Angeles on one tank of any fuel. They'll get 150 to 400 miles per gallon, and could possibly get much more. The hypercar burns 100 or even 1,000 times cleaner than present cars. Hypercars will be sturdier, safer, sportier, more comfortable, beautiful, durable, and quiet—and just generally *nicer* than present cars. They may even cost less.

But they're profoundly different in many ways, and therefore, come up against cultural barriers within the automaking industry. Also, though hypercars buy us time, they cannot solve the transportation problem, and, indeed, may make it worse, by making driving even cheaper and more attractive than it is now.

How is this all possible? First, let me spend just a minute on the physics of cars. Despite decades of devoted incremental effort by Detroit, only about 15 percent to 20 percent of gas tank fuel energy still ever manages to reach the wheels. Why is that? Cars are conventionally made of steel. Steel is heavy. It takes a lot of force to accelerate something heavy, so conventional cars need enormous engines, engines so oversized that their average efficiency is cut in half. The energy that does reach the wheels is dissipated in three roughly equal shares in city driving: heating the air that the car pushes aside, heating the tires and road, and heating the brakes when you stop. In other words, one-third of the delivered wheel-power in a conventional car goes to heat the air, one-third to heat the tires and road, and one-third to heat the brakes.

The ultralight strategy is to make the car several-fold lighter (yet safer, too); make it two-and-a-half to six times more slippery so that it can cut through the air; and reduce the tire and road heating by a factor of 3 to 5. Hypercar tires are about twice as good as the best radials, which is not bad to begin with. Finally, the electric drive motors can convert motion back into heat, recovering 70 percent of the braking energy for reuse.

Basically, the hypercar is designed like an airplane rather than a tank. The outside is smaller. The inside is bigger. I call it state-of-the-shelf technology. The skin or shell of the car is made of glass, Kevlar, and even carbon fibers—very light, very expensive, but so little is used, it makes less of a difference than you might think. When you put the family inside with the suitcases and the dog, the payload will weigh more than the car.

The hybrid-electric drive part of the hypercar means that the wheels are driven mostly or wholly by electricity. The hypercar would not be battery driven because fuel has 100 times as much energy per pound as batteries. Rather, the hypercar would use a tiny engine, gas turbine, or other conversion device, to make electricity on board as needed for propulsion.

Let me make this a little more real. A plain old ultralight prototype has already been built. It is called the "GM Ultralite." Two copies were built in 1991 by fifty people in 100 days at General Motors at a cost of about 4 to 6 million dollars, which was equivalent to about eight hours' worth of the company's North American losses at that time. Inside, it's as big as a Corsica. Outside, it's as small as a Miata. It weighs 1,400 pounds, including four airbags. The shell is light carbon fiber (though it could be a lot lighter). The engine is a tiny little thing, smaller than a Honda Civic engine, and yet it matches the acceleration of a 12-cylinder BMW—zero to sixty in 7.8

seconds—because it's so light. Top speed is 135 miles per hour. You can go directly to jail on any highway on earth.

Amory believes Detroit is halfway there with the Ultralite, but may not make it up the hill. Too many cultural barriers.

Imagine that the Big Three typewriter makers—like the Big Three car makers—were about one-seventh of the U.S. Gross National Product, directly and indirectly. You remember typewriters, don't you? Over the decades, typewriter makers have gone from manual to electric, and let's say they're now working on the subtle incremental refinements for the forthcoming Selectric 17. These are good typewriters, the Selectric 17's. The Big Three probably sell 12 million of them a year. There's only one little problem coming over the horizon. Namely, the competition is working on wireless subnotebook computers.

This is where the steel-car industry is today. It is exquisitely sophisticated and good at what it does. It is the highest expression of the Iron Age. And it is fundamentally obsolete.

The big automakers start with two disadvantages, as energy expert Lee Schipper said: they're big and they're automakers. It's really tough to change a die-making, steel-stamping culture into a molded-synthetics, electronics, and software culture. What I'm discussing is really much more like a computer with wheels than it is like a car with chips. Maybe the companies that will do it best will not be automakers at all, but the Hewlett-Packards of the world, the systems integrators who learn fast.

Not many people in Detroit understand something we should have learned from the wreckage of IBM's mainframe computer business: that you have to kill your own products with better new products before someone else does. As they say at 3M, "We'd rather eat our own lunch, thank you."

If you don't take risks, Amory believes, you may be put out of business by the first corporation that leapfrogs, thereby turning Detroit's incremental improvements strategy into a bet-your-company strategy. "That competitor may not be Honda," he adds. "It may be a bunch of smart, hungry aerospace engineers in a garage in Southern California, or Northern Italy, or Switzerland, people you've never heard of, who are off your radar, the next Apple."

Now, at this point, I should say I only acquired my first Apple PowerBook at age eighty-two. We recently had two cars, my wife and I—a 1983 Toyota, and a 1968 Volvo with 267,000 miles on it. There are only 160,000 on the Toyota, and the Volvo just went to the glue factory. I am ready for a hypercar. But is the world?

In some respects, yes. We're paying $50 billion a year for oil imports in this country alone. Factor in the cost of keeping the peacetime army in trim, so that it is always ready to intervene in the Persian Gulf and protect the sludge at the wellhead, and the cost of oil becomes very expensive indeed. Amory points out that about three-fifths of the air pollution in this country puffs and spurts from one-fifth of our cars. If we made the switch to hypercars, there would be a lot less pollution and we would all save a lot of fuel dollars. Since Amory's hypercars are more reliable and simpler to fix, the mechanic can just come out to your house. Since they can be manufactured quickly, requiring no years of expensive retooling, you'll probably be able to order one by phone. They'll build it when they receive your check, and send it out—like L. L. Bean, only on a bigger truck. There is no need for a hypercar sales force. Over half the people involved in making and selling today's cars, and about a third of the price, can be chalked up to the old way of showrooming automobiles.

This little revolution is going to put a few people out of work, especially if Detroit wakes up as slowly as it did to my buying cars from Volkswagen, Toyota, and Volvo, and giving up on Ford, Mercury, Pontiac, Buick, and Chevrolet. Amory informs me that the United States is ahead in all the relevant technology, however. As far as "the national interest" is concerned, the future could swing either way. "There are," says Amory, raising his eyebrows, "unique opportunities, let us say, for rapid market entry"—then he smiles—"and rapid market exit" on the part of the steel-car companies.

"Ready or not," concludes my friend Amory Lovins, "we're all about to embark on one of the greatest adventures in industrial history."

Are environmentalists ready? The implications for them are as strong as they are for car manufacturers. We won't be in danger of running out of oil anymore, or at least for a much longer time, and our air stands a chance of becoming much cleaner. But we will run out of roads and pavement, because so many more people in so many more countries will be able to afford hypercars. And what will this mean for rapid transit outside urban areas? The beautiful curse of the automobile will not leave us. Environmentalists were right about cars in the first place. What we will need in the era of the hypercar, then more than ever, is less automobility through better land-use policies. Those cities with boundaries that I mentioned earlier, which put work closer to home and leave the Big Outside restored and wild, must become bare necessity, if we are all not to be flattened by the future. Let the car be a pet, not a workhorse.

PART III

Restoration

CHAPTER II

A World Restored

Latent in the restoration movement, we can imagine a
potential not simply to change the direction of Western
culture but to alter its foundation.

—Barry Lopez

BROKEN EGGS must remain broken, but broken hearts
may be mended with love. Extinct species are gone, but
endangered plants and animals may be brought back from the
brink. Exhausted fields can renew themselves. Grass can annihi-
late pavement. So long as life lasts, dashed hopes stand a chance.
We need only get over that current feeling that says, "Where
there is life there must be hopelessness." We must ever answer
the question "But what can I do?" with the realization that
restoring the Earth, making things better, renews and heals us at
the same time.

Restoration is a deceptively complex concept. It means re-
generation. Return the natural world to the way it was, as best
we can, before clearcutting, acid mining, inelegant development,

pollution, and the industrial accidents of bygone eras harmed the Earth. Give nature a jump start, and stand back.

Restoration means putting the Earth's life-support systems back in working order: rivers, forests, wetlands, deserts, soil, and endangered species, too. Many dams on many rivers have been made unnecessary by new systems of energy generation and distribution. Let's take out those superfluous dams, beginning with Yosemite's Hetch Hetchy, which never should have been dammed. We need forests, not just tree plantations. Wetlands, as we are beginning to learn, purify our drinking water, acting like giant filters. Ducks like them, too. Deserts require reclamation, not inundation. And isn't it about time we stopped treating soil like dirt?

Human systems also need restoration. Let's rehabilitate the South Bronx, and all the other places like it across the Earth. To accomplish that, we must give the unemployed and the never-employed a stake in the wider restoration process. Let's also put environmental conscience into world trade and into our corporate thinking. It is time corporations moved from green public relations to green operations, so far as their environmental strategy is concerned. Restoration departments should be added to whatever Departments of the Interior are called the world around, and to the World Bank, while eco-spin—meaning that you carry on with your work, but you carry on with the best interests of the Earth as you do so—should be included in every thinking person's job description, from farmer to architect.

Of late, there has been an epidemic of cynicism, a general inability to understand how right Richard Barnet was when he said, "We march toward annihilation under the banner of Realism."

Whatever and whoever has brought humanity to the edge of the chasm probably just thought they were being practical. Practical people, as has been pointed out, are those who have made all their decisions, lost the ability to listen, and are determined to perpetuate the errors of their ancestors. They have all the foresight implicit in this advice: "When you reach the fork in the road, take it."

More people need to understand that milk does not come from a plastic container, or water from a valve, or gasoline from a throttle. The sources of human wealth have been provided for by nature on the only planet most of us are ever likely to reside upon comfortably. The Earth's ecological capital has been sorely overdrawn. We are running out of the things that fuel economic growth.

"If today is a typical day on the planet Earth," writes environmental scientist David W. Orr in *Earth in Mind*, "we will lose 116 square miles of rain forest, or about an acre a second. We will lose another 72 square miles to encroaching deserts, the results of human mismanagement and overpopulation. We will lose 40 to 250 species, and no one knows whether the number is 40 or 250. Today the human population will increase by 250,000. And today we will add 2,700 tons of chlorofluorocarbons and 15 million tons of carbon dioxide to the atmosphere. Tonight the Earth will be a little hotter, its waters more acidic, and the fabric of life more threadbare."

HARD-CORE statistics like Orr's are an essential wake-up call. I have a younger friend named Severn Cullis-Suzuki, who spoke at the plenary session of Earth Summit in Rio de Janeiro in June 1992, when she was twelve years old. This was the speech the future vice president, Al Gore, liked best of all, according to biologist David Suzuki, her father. I can think of nothing more important to restoration than the restoration of hope in children. I show the video of her wake-up call every time I get the chance:[1]

Hello, I'm Severn Suzuki. . . .

Coming up here today, I have no hidden agenda. I am fighting for my future. Losing my future is not like losing an election or a few points on the stock market. . . .

I am afraid to go out in the sun now because of the holes in the ozone. I am afraid to breathe the air because I don't know what chemicals are in it. I used to go fishing in Vancouver with my dad until just a few years ago we found the fish full of cancers. And now we hear about animals and plants becoming extinct every day—vanishing forever.

---

[1]The full text and story appear in a beautifully illustrated children's book, *Tell the World: A Young Environmentalist Speaks Out*, by Severn Cullis-Suzuki (Doubleday Canada Limited, 1993).

In my life, I have dreamed of seeing the great herds of wild animals, jungles and rainforests full of birds and butterflies, but now I wonder if they will even exist for my children to see. Did you have to worry about these little things when you were my age?

All this is happening before our eyes and yet we act as if we have all the time we want and all the solutions. I'm only a child and I don't have all the solutions, but I want you to realize, neither do you!

You don't know how to fix the holes in our ozone layer.

You don't know how to bring salmon back up a dead stream.

You don't know how to bring back an animal now extinct.

And you can't bring back the forests that once grew where there is now desert.

If you don't know how to fix it, please stop breaking it!

Here you may be delegates of your governments, businesspeople, organizers, reporters, or politicians. But really you are mothers and fathers, sisters and brothers, aunts and uncles. And each of you is somebody's child. . . .

Two days ago here in Brazil, we were shocked when we spent some time with some children living on the streets. . . .

I can't stop thinking that these children are my own age, and that it makes a tremendous difference where you are born. I could be one of those children living in the *favellas* of Rio. I could be a child starving in Somalia, a victim of war in the Middle East or a beggar in India.

I'm only a child yet I know if all the money spent on war was spent on ending poverty and finding environmental answers, what a wonderful place this Earth would be.

At school, even in kindergarten, you teach us to behave in the world. You teach us:

not to fight with others

to work things out

to respect others

to clean up our mess

not to hurt other creatures

to share, not to be greedy.

Then why do you go out and do the things you tell us not to do?

Parents should be able to comfort their children by saying, "Everything's going to be all right"; "We're doing the best we can" and "It's not the end of the world." But I don't think you can say that to us anymore. Are we even on your list of priorities?

My dad always says, "You are what you do, not what you say."

Well, what you do makes me cry at night.

You grown-ups say you love us. I challenge you, *please*, make your actions reflect your words.

Thank you for listening.

I BELIEVE some adults were listening in 1992. It was a year that the world seemed to examine itself, like a marble held in a child's hand, something we had not done since the first moon landing or the original Earth Day. In 1992 more than 2,000 concerned scientists spoke out. Perhaps they had heard Severn. Among these scientists were 102 Nobel laureates:

> No more than one or a few decades remain before the chance to avert the threats we now confront will be lost and the prospects for humanity immeasurably diminished. A new ethic is required, a new attitude toward discharging our responsibility for caring for ourselves and for the earth. This ethic must motivate a great movement, convincing reluctant leaders and reluctant peoples themselves to effect needed change.

It is time to visualize that proper new ethic. It is time to reweave life's fragile web. It is time, finally, to begin to restore what we and our "practical" ancestors have so carelessly destroyed.

By restoring the Earth, we have the opportunity to invest in ecological sanity, to reinvest in prosperity, to invest in an understanding of how nature works and what we have to do to let it work. It is healing time on Earth. Of course, we should not be so arrogant as to think that we've got all the answers, because we haven't. If we're not careful, we could make the old mistakes, such as bringing rabbits to Australia, the mongoose to Hawaii, or something perhaps even worse, like a chemical overdose to the human fetus on its fifty-sixth day, when its decision to be male or female can be confused.

As an economic engine, restoration will prove to be a boon to the economies of the world. It is a movement, already begun, that I believe will come to involve millions of people, young and old, in what I have called CPR for the Earth—Conservation, Preservation, and Restoration. I hope it will also engage the great religions, savvy armies, and powerful corporations both altruistic and shrewd. After all that, even governments might follow.

I started out as a boy bent over a spring. Then I climbed mountains. I became a conservationist. Then I saw what we all were doing, and I wanted to stop us from doing worse. Now I want to restore what once was, not for an old man's memories, but for a baby's smile.

CHAPTER 12

Making a Difference

The wilderness holds answers to more questions
than we have yet learned how to ask.

—Nancy Newhall

SOMETIMES IT SEEMS to me the restoration movement
started itself. Perhaps the Earth whispered Aldo Leopold's
"goose music" into the ears of isolated individuals, and they were
moved by the honking. Perhaps things had got so bad in some
places that certain men and women just wanted it put back the
way it was, and possessed the visionary moxie to do the putting,
to see restoration through. These individuals are like travelers lost
in the wild, who want to go back to the last recognizable land-
mark and look again for the next. Restoration is not an effort to
stop the clock, but rather a chance to keep the clock running—in
fact, our best chance.

In the last two or three decades, people, like seeds, have
planted themselves in ravaged terrain and begun to do some

work—from Bermuda's Nonesuch Island to the despoiled Matt-hole River of Northern California, to the moonscape of Auroville in India, to the banks of the Nashua River in New Hampshire, to the urban war zones of the South Bronx, to the cement quarries of Kenya, to the polluted Neva River of the old Soviet Union and the "living dead" that Dan Janzen found in the scattered bi-otic debris of the dry tropical forest of Costa Rica, as I'll explain in a minute. Without fanfare, these unlinked humans have begun to make a difference. They are fixing the soil, bringing back the salmon and the not-quite-extinct cahow, and helping the homeless to help themselves.

Some pretty big projects are being undertaken. Money is being raised and money is being spent, generating jobs and sus-taining careers as well as regenerating the trashed Earth. Major new players, a new breed of engineering firm and a new type of green corporation, have begun to fly on the side of the angels. A new field of endeavor has been created, with hydrologists and botanists changing things for the good. There is now a restoration industry, and "systemic problems rather than symptoms are being addressed," as John Berger puts it. The return of the meandering Kissimmee, or what most people would call the saving of the Florida Everglades, is an example of what can happen when indi-vidual obsession steamrolls politicians, and everybody suddenly discovers they are doing the right thing, by themselves and by the Earth, and at the same time.

I had heard about some of these efforts, small and big, when I was president of Friends of the Earth. But I first began to fathom the significance of what was happening—that our species was finally, spontaneously, and gloriously making a U-turn—after I read two remarkable books, *Restoring the Earth*, by John Berger, and *Helping Nature Heal*, edited by Richard Nilsen.

What follows are a few examples that I like to savor, of regenerating soil, islands, forests, and rivers.

Alan Lithman begins his account of "Revisiting Auroville" in *Helping Nature Heal*:

We were dragging our bicycles across the barren fields avoiding the sharp stubble, all that was left by the migrant herds of cows and goats. A merciless sun beat down upon this wretched piece of earth, bleaching it bone white or a brittle terra-cotta. A once-living earth dying back into a moon. We reached the edge of a canyon whose fingers gouged through the landscape. My friend pointed across the ravine to the barren plateau beyond, where a few palmyra trees shimmered like phantoms in the heat waves. "There it is," he said, "Auroville." I looked and saw nothing but a vacant landscape that slid into the Bay of Bengal. How could I possibly live there? How could anyone?

This was how Tamil Nadu in southern India looked in 1969, denuded by generations of subsistence agriculturists. Twenty-five years later, more than two million indigenous trees have been planted. A soft lip of forest greens the sunsets. I was taken with a diagram of how cleverly those trees were planted. A square hole was dug into barren rock with a *mumpti*, what we might call a garden adz. The cube shape induced the roots to grow into the corners, so they would not circle around themselves. Trees planted on hillsides were dug with a groove in the mulched rim so that rainwater naturally flowed down to them, and was caught.

But I was struck as much by Lithman's philosophical understanding of what was going on as by his practical wisdom:

We have all been colonialists on this planet. At Auroville, there was simply no buffer with which to fool ourselves. [They were down to laterite, rock without soil, a bad spot to be in, if you want to grow things.] It was clear what had to be done, and there was no one else to do it for us. We were humanity coming home to repay a terrestrial debt from the West to the East, a karma that we owed to the earth.

DAVID WINGATE began his Caribbean restoration project a long time ago, before even Auroville. As a schoolboy on Bermuda, he had an unusual interest in birds. His precocious enthusiasm caused him to be invited on a passionate expedition in the late 1940s to discover if there were any cahows still alive. The cahow is a Caribbean seabird, a type of petrel related to the albatross. Cahows were thought to have checked out in the 1600s when the Spanish and British decimated this part of the Caribbean by introducing pigs and logging the original cedar forests for shipbuilding.

Here is how Wingate describes their rediscovery: "I will never forget the elation on Dr. Murphy's face when he and Mowbray succeeded in noosing a bird out of its deep nesting crevice, held it up to the light, and exclaimed, 'By Gad, the cahow!'"

By Gad, the cahow! I laughed when I read that. But I wonder why no one laughs when the *New York Times* reports that there are now 360 billionaires in the world, 200 of them in the United States. Somewhere along the line we have misplaced our priorities. David Wingate is a saint, more so than St. Francis, who only allowed the squirrels to sit upon his lap. Wingate took a certain knowledge of biology and set about to rebuild the ecosystem of Nonesuch Island, planting 8,000 trees by himself, taking out the introduced rats with warfarin, nurturing old plant and animal species still around from precolonial times, hand-feeding the nestlings of the yellow-crowned night heron with chopped-up land crabs. He has created a living museum of what once was, and could be, again.

Nonesuch Island. Such a beautiful name. There will be many more such places.

FOR SEVEN YEARS I have been unable to make a speech without talking about Daniel Janzen of the University of Pennsylvania, the ecological consultant to Fundación Neotrópica, in San Jose, Costa Rica. The beginning of his article in *Science*, "Tropical Ecological and Biocultural Restoration," always scares me, though his solutions cheer me. This important paper begins:

> The increasingly vigorous efforts to protect some of the relatively intact portions of tropical nature come too late and too slow for well over half the tropics—especially the half best suited to agriculture and animal husbandry. Its relatively intact habitats are gone. Its remaining wildlands are hardly more than scattered biotic debris. The only feasible next step is conservation of biodiversity by using the living biotic debris and inocula from nearby intact areas to restore habitats. If this step is not taken quickly, natural and anthropogenic perturbations will extinguish most of the habitat remnants, small population fragments, and the living dead—the organisms that are living out their physiological life spans, but are no longer members of persistent populations.

Who has scattered this "biotic debris," in which Janzen includes the "living dead"? You and I and our time on Earth.

Janzen explains how restoration may be jump-started, and how he has begun to accomplish this necessary miracle himself.

First, there must be "an adequate inoculum of plants and animals," and these must be "permitted to invade and grow":

Choose an appropriate site, obtain it, and hire some of the former users as live-in managers. Sort through the habitat remnants to see which can recover. Stop the biotic and physical challenges to those remnants. The challenge is to turn the farmer's skills at biomanipulation to work for the conservation of biodiversity. . . .

Human cultures evolved in mutualism and conflict with the natural world. . . . Tropical humans are experiencing nearly total loss of this integral part of their mental lives. It is as though they are losing their color vision and most of their hearing.

AS NANCY NEWHALL wrote in *This Is the American Earth*, the first of the Sierra Club's exhibit-format books, inspired by Ansel Adams: "The wilderness holds answers to more questions than we have yet learned how to ask."

At our peril do we pulp and shred those answers. If in all too many places all that is left are scattered biotic debris and the living dead, we had better begin to join them together once more, to restore them in order to restore our own minds as well.

Large ecosystems, once wild, may also undergo the process. It is instructive to consider the Everglades. To settlers in Florida, the Everglades were a useless wasteland that frustrated their efforts to raise cattle and sugarcane. Anything that could be done to remove the threat of flooding and transform the swampy prairie into pasture was deserving of unqualified support. The heart of the whole messy system was the Kissimmee River, a sluggish body of water that could not be easily controlled.

In the 1960s the Army Corps of Engineers straightened the kinks in the Kissimmee, shortening the river from 97 miles to 54. A canal was built down the middle, straight as a crow's flight and longer. The old meandering oxbows were left to bleach in the Florida sun, along with millions of animals and rare plants, among them wading birds, alligators, deer, and Florida panthers. Soon the purity of the water at the bottom end of the state, serving major cities, turned bad. It seems that the useless floodplain of the Everglades had served as one of those giant filtering fans, slowly cleansing the sheet of water as it flowed south, recharging the aquifer. The only thing gained was, in effect, enormous subsidies for sugar corporations and cattle growers—and a river flowing faster than it was designed to flow.

In the 1970s the losses to cities through degraded drinking water became politically obvious. Everglades that were drying up were also becoming far less attractive to tourists, and tourism had become an industry ten times bigger than sugar and cattle, a story being repeated across the world.

In the 1980s the Sierra Club, the Audubon Society, and a small army of volunteers joined with rising Florida politicians such as Bob Graham, who would become a U.S. Senator, to restore the Everglades. Steel weirs were built across the upper Kissimmee Canal, which slowed the flow and backed water into the old oxbows. Once again, the water was cleaned by natural processes, grasses, and settling. Herons, alligators, and panthers have begun their return.

Graham's goal by the year 2000 is to have the Everglades look and function the way they did in 1900.

SOME FARSIGHTED people are thinking about restoring another large ecosystem, the "buffalo commons." Many counties on the Great Plains and in arid regions of eastern Montana and the Dakotas are not doing so well agriculturally. They rarely have done well, except in years of unusually high rains. Perhaps these places would work better the old way, with buffalo restored to the tall grass with which they coevolved. Coevolution requires a symbiotic relationship that I believe buffalo could handle and cows don't. Far from removing humans from these areas, a buffalo commons might provide new eco-tourist dollars for depressed small towns. Humans would cluster themselves outside the buffalo reserves, just as they do now within agricultural centers.

The bison would move among the restored areas, along wildlife corridors. Imagine: bison underpasses below the occasional human interstate. In Berkeley's Tilden Park, we have signs on the roadway that say "Newt Crossing" and have even closed a park road during the mating season to allow the newts to cross safely in the essential search of each for the other.

Should I tell Congressman Gingrich about this?

CHAPTER 13

The CPR Service

We travel together, passengers on a little space ship,
dependent upon its vulnerable reserves of air and soil, all
committed for our safety to its security and place, preserved
from annihilation only by the care, the work and, I will say,
the love we give our fragile craft.

We cannot maintain it half fortunate, half miserable, half
confident, half despairing, half slave to the ancient enemies of
mankind and half free in a liberation of resources undreamed
of until this day. No craft, no crew, can travel safely with such
vast contradictions. On their resolution depends the security
of us all.

—Adlai Stevenson, July 1965

FROM TIME immemorial, our kind has fought wars.
But we cannot have peace *on* the Earth without making peace
with the Earth. I was a combat veteran of World War II, the war
Studs Terkel called "the last good war." I entered as a private,
retired as a major, and had a hand in teaching ten thousand
younger men to climb mountains. Before too long, other young
men would be shooting at them, and they needed to know how

to handle rough terrain as well as the enemy when the time came.

Just before the war's end, the Germans were retreating across the Po Valley. When you retreat, tactics require that you leave some soldiers with sharp eyes behind as snipers. They have a tough job. If they don't do it well, the troops may be overtaken and destroyed. If they do it too well for too long, they can't rejoin their own outfit and may be captured. Our men caught such a sniper. He had killed one of us, and men who fight beside each other are like brothers.

I was the battalion intelligence officer, and the sniper was brought back to me. I knew what the rules were. He was a prisoner of war. I should have immediately said something like, "Take the son of a bitch back to regiment."

But I hesitated, and in that pause the buddy of the man who had been killed shot the sniper. We searched the dead man's pockets. Inside were pictures of the wife and children he would never see because I had hesitated.

In life, as in the wilderness, as I would learn a decade later with Glen Canyon, you must know the situation you are in and act in time.

You don't forget something like that easily. I prefer to remember what happened two nights after we received word that World War II was over. My battalion became part of a regimental combat team that was told to go from Lake Garda to Passo de Resia on the Austrian border. When night fell beyond Merano, we turned on blackout lights from habit. But blackout lights don't light anything up worth a damn. I got a bright idea, and called on the radio to our commanding officer. This was Lt. Col. John Hay, who later would become a four-star general:

"Jack, why are we driving blackout? The war is over."

The colonel came back, "You got a point, Dave," and gave the command, "Turn on your lights, men."

They did, all along the four-mile column.

Our scouts found out that the Germans on the pass didn't know the war was over. Their artillery was laid on us, and they were about to fire when we lit up. Assuming that we knew something that they didn't know, they held their fire. They understood what the sudden turning on of our lights meant: that the war was over. I proclaimed myself a hero for having suggested that we turn our lights on.

The war against the Earth should also be over. It is time that we turn on the lights globally.

AS A FORMER military officer and a current observer of our amusing species, I am not so ingenuous as to believe that armed force will not be needed to police the errant of the world at least until Paradise arrives in the arms of Ecotopia and Sin has finally left the planet. Nevertheless, the Cold War has wound down, and there are some big armies out there, America's included. They have the technical know-how, the training, and the dedication to service needed to redesign human systems and restore natural systems—our ecological capital. What to do, now that peace has broken out?

And what, as well, to motivate inner-city youth? General Alfred Gray, former commandant of the U.S. Marine Corps, believes, "The greatest threat to national security is the combination of crime, drugs, lost educational opportunities, and the economic consequences of these failures." The army of the unemployed and a land badly in need of shoulder-to-shoulder restoring should be introduced to each other.

Recently, my eye caught some lines from Stewart Brand, the former military officer who gave us the original *Whole Earth Catalog*: "My platoon could have made short work of restoring a salmon stream, assisting a controlled forest burn, helping protect African wildlife from poachers, or planting native shrubs at the edge of a growing desert. I wonder if they might get this opportunity."

Brand adds: "Natural systems are priceless in value and nearly impossible to replace, but they're cheap to maintain. All you have to do is defend them."

Increasingly, intelligent and dedicated military men the world over are concluding, as has Brigadier Michael Harbottle, OBE, a former senior officer of NATO, that "the environment probably poses the greatest threat to the security and to the survival of the human race."

I alluded earlier to Robert D. Kaplan's strong conclusion in "The Coming Anarchy," printed in 1994 in the *Atlantic Monthly*:

It is time to understand "the environment" for what it is: the national-security issue of the early twenty-first century. The political and strategic impact of surging populations, spreading disease, deforestation and soil erosion, water depletion, air pollution, and, possibly, rising sea levels in critical, overcrowded regions like the Nile Delta and Bangladesh—developments that will prompt mass migrations and, in turn, incite group conflicts—will be the core foreign-policy challenge from which most others will ultimately emanate.

Not only those remote regions, but Florida and California as well. I would add, with more hope, that anarchy need not reign. Deforestation, species extinction, soil erosion, water depletion, and air pollution are problems environmentalists have had good solutions to for some time. The Earth can be healed. This is what restoration is all about. It is time for all policymakers to wake up.

Recently, I generously offered the whole Pentagon building to an EPA audience: "If you add Restoration to your Protection mission, you will add more to global security than the Pentagon does." I haven't told the Pentagon yet.

The duty of armed forces is to serve their country. Our country, like most countries, is in danger from within, in the coming decades, from what we have done to ourselves, what we have destroyed. The Army Corps of Engineers once dammed and channelized our rivers with great skill. Remember the Kissimmee?

Industry required an end to the Everglades, or thought it did. It is time for army and Bureau of Reclamation engineers to restore our rivers instead of trickling and dribbling them, as a Native American puts it. I think, being good citizens, the engineers may well want to. Government should listen.

WHEN I MAKE speeches, I ask how many people in the audience would be willing to commit at least one year of their lives out of the next ten to working to restore the Earth. They could work for pay or as a volunteer, somewhere in the world, as close as the nearest mountain or the nearest poor urban area, as far away as the country of their dreams. Almost always, two-thirds of the audience raise their hands (I've asked almost 350,000 people so far). To demonstrate the vulnerability of polls, I ask the question again in a different way: How many would be unwilling? Rarely does a hand go up. "So it's unanimous," I tell them. "Let's go!"

People want to help, but there is no organization for them to join, certainly nothing coordinated on a global level that is dedicated to restoring the Earth, at least until our armies expand their role.

I am old enough to remember another corps: the Civilian Conservation Corps (CCC), under Franklin Roosevelt, during the Great Depression. It was particularly un-depressing to camp in the woods, shore up overgrazed stream banks, replant the prairies, and sleep around a campfire under a full moon (think of it: a full moon every twenty-eight days), or listen to the goose music overhead as you worked hard to save the geese. The CCC created forty-four wildlife refuges in this country and set 2 billion trees in the ground. Three million Americans were given jobs.

There should be an "Earth Corps" or perhaps a "CPR Corps" that would take up where the Peace Corps left off, and be fully concerned with endangered species and the endangered Earth. That's what Sam LaBudde proposed, in a moment between the campaign for dolphin-safe tuna and the equally successful campaign to stop drift-netters from strip-mining the high seas of fish.

A CPR Corps would help to solve the problem of the unemployed, but it would also enlist the highly employable. How many hydraulic engineers would truly love to jump the catwalk and restore rivers rather than build dams, perhaps even use their skills to rip out unnecessary dams, and get those salmon jumping again for joy? How many biologists might bolt the universities for a year, given the chance to show us all how it should be done? How many MBAs might welcome a chance, using intuition, to show what failure to invest in maintenance and replacement costs the Earth? Under a starry night sky, of course.

Our innovative scheme is to add a CPR component to other organizations, from the Peace Corps to the armed forces, from 3M to GM to the local ditch-digging company, from what is taught in kindergarten to what can be practiced in elder hostels, from regular columns in local papers to what a Bill Moyers can do on television, or what Bill Clinton can do if he stops being buffaloed by Bob Dole and Newt Gingrich and gives us a series of eloquent fireside chats about what he will be doing for global CPR, that will give them, him, and us a chance.

No one budget can possibly pay for all the CPR the Earth so desperately needs. But with a certain sleight of hand, the funds can be found in already existing budgets of every government bureau and in each corporation, as well. CPR would be added to everybody's job description. That is, one of your finest duties would be to keep our life-support system alive, by restoring it. Call it a mandatory form of life insurance, like breathing and circulating your blood.

The CPR Corps, under various jurisdictions and as part of every budget, would work like an international Green Cross. Just as the Red Cross repairs the hurt and damage done to people in nature's wilder moments, the CPR Corps would bind the wounds and repair the damage people have done to the Earth.

Medically, CPR means cardiopulmonary resuscitation, getting the heart and lungs back in working order, with thump and mouth. That's what we need to do with the Earth: put it back in good order. Starting now.

The acronym CPR, you'll remember, stands for: Conservation, Preservation, and Restoration. I'd add Celebration, but it spoils the acronym.

You can sum it up with a ten-second sound bite: Conserve the golden eggs carefully. Preserve the goose or there will be no more golden eggs. If you've already damaged the goose, get going on restoration.

We would conserve by using our natural capital rationally. We haven't been all that reasonable lately. We would preserve what we cannot replace—the planet's biodiversity. If you can't replace something, then you'd better preserve it. Save all the parts. And we would restore by rebuilding, enlisting science and technology in generating rather than ripping apart the Earth's resources.

The one critical ingredient that has been missing is compassion. A CPR effort would build on compassion toward the Earth. And it will be fun.

The longer I've been here, the better I like this planet. We might just as well stop beating it, and get about healing the wounds no species but our own has inflicted.

CPR!

Restore!

CHAPTER 14

What Will It Cost?

To move ahead to a restorative economy, the industrial
corporations of the world must change to meet the world's
needs, not the other way around.

—Paul Hawken

NATURALLY, people are worried about the taxing and
spending that will be required to pay the cost of restoring our
eco-structure, but we've been borrowing and spending ecological
capital—and deferring maintenance and replacement—since the
beginning of the Industrial Revolution. My idea of budgeting is
to ask, What will it cost if we don't do it? Once you pay to restore a forest or a river or a spot of blighted ground, you suddenly
understand how much it was worth in the first place. You're
much less likely to trash the Earth in the future.

In fact, once the idea of restoration takes hold, there is big
money to be made. If you don't think there is, try taking your car
to the shop, or your body to the doctor, and find out who's making money. You're glad to pay, too. Your car works better. You feel

better and will live longer. The Earth is not so different. There is something fundamentally wrong with treating the planet as if it were a business in liquidation.

Riparian restorations in and about California's cities sometimes cost $6,000 or more an acre. It is always cheaper to imagine what the cost to the Earth will be before we pollute, but those who are paid to clean up society's messes pay taxes, buy groceries, and vote, too, just like defense workers. The Southern Pacific Railroad, to its credit, spent millions to clean up the Sacramento River after a tank car full of herbicide derailed in the mountains near Dunsmuir. Hard-rock mining companies, which in this country often receive a free ride—or giveaway—from the antiquated 1872 Mining Law, can, should, and sometimes do tax themselves to reclaim the lands they destroy in the process of providing our gold jewelry and chrome, as well as more central metals.

There is also big money to be saved, once you understand how to solve the problem before it starts. In *The Ecology of Commerce*, my friend Paul Hawken, who founded Smith & Hawken, describes a delightful achievement of the 3M Company:

> To move ahead to a restorative economy, the industrial corporations of the world must change to meet the world's needs, not the other way around. . . . In 1975, Joseph Ling, head of 3M's environmental department, developed a program called Pollution Prevention Pays (3P),

the first integrated, intracompany approach to designing out pollution from manufacturing processes. The plan created incentives for the technical staff to modify product manufacturing methods so as to prevent hazardous and toxic waste, and to reduce costs. By reformulating products, changing processes, redesigning equipment, and recovering waste for reuse or recycling, 3M has been able to save $537 million. During the fifteen-year period, it reduced its air pollution by 120,000 tons, its wastewater by one billion gallons, its solid waste by 410,000 tons. Over 3,000 separate initiatives have contributed to the cause, and the key to the whole enterprise was a strong mandate from the top management of the corporation, linked with on-going support and assistance to line employees. In 1986, 3M expanded the scope of the program with a goal to eliminate 90 percent of all emissions by the end of this decade, and to achieve zero emissions sometime after that. Not only does this prevent material from entering the waste stream, it garners sales and therefore income for what was once an expense.

Paul has another idea for restoration from the start. Let Sony, for instance, retain title to the TV it leases or sells you, and have the company take it back when it stops working. No one could possibly know better how to disassemble it, reuse the reusable parts, and properly dispose of the toxic ones. In due course, the companies would learn to design the way nature does in nature's cradle-to-cradle scheme. Everything must be recyclable: TVs, refrigerators, cars, all goods currently disposable.

The 3M Company did the right thing by the Earth. The problem of the corporation, especially the multinational, is that it is given the rights of a person without conscience. Somehow, we've got to build conscience back into the corporate structure. When I say "we," I mean consumers, customers, executives, stockholders, and employees. Corporations have the organizational ability. They have the money. They have the political power. But they've got to realize that there will be no corporations, no stockholders, no profits, and no sex on a dead planet. The Fortune 500 must be brought into the restoration movement. Otherwise, it won't happen. Time is running out, fast.

Those corporate directors who understand that their grandchildren will live on the Earth after them have already made the U-turn. Green business is big, and getting much bigger. I am always heartened by companies such as Ben & Jerry's, Body Shop, Esprit, Gap, Levi Strauss, Patagonia, Real Goods, Smith & Hawken, and 3M, and their often much larger counterparts in Europe. There is such a thing as the consumer vote, as the writers of economic textbooks are so fond of citing. It should be wielded with vigilance by environmentalists, who must understand who is doing what to the Earth, and buy accordingly. When that is apparent, things have a way of changing overnight. Those dolphin-catching tuna companies changed, and so did Nestlé, Gallo,

Burger King, and McDonald's, in their various experiments with Styrofoam containers, rain-forest beef, and pesticides. Many other corporations might enjoy the consumer support that the public's embrace of restoration and right-living will bring, as well as corrective subsidies.

As a small spur to progress, I would like to publish a book with the title, *The Misfortune 500*. Each page would have a picture of what a misdirected company had done to the Earth, a before-and-after illustration. However, since corporations all over the world are now making that U-turn, the book would have two parts, and it would be reissued every two years. The good companies effecting change would move up front, until the back of the book grew thinner and thinner. Finally, the back section would contain just one blank, white page.

That would be my idea of a good read.

CHAPTER 15

The Cure for What Ails Us

I seek acquaintance with nature—to know her moods and
manners. Primitive nature is the most interesting to me.
I take infinite pains to know all the phenomena of spring,
for instance, thinking that I have here the entire poem, and
then, to my chagrin, I learn that it is but an imperfect copy
that I possess and have read, that my ancestors have torn out
many of the first leaves and grandest passages, and mutilated
it in many places. I should not like to think that some demigod
had come before me and picked out some of the best of the
stars. I wish to know an entire heaven and an entire Earth.

—Henry David Thoreau, *Journals*, March 23, 1856

ONLY A FEW years ago, I was flying nonstop from
Kuwait to Los Angeles. At one point I was bored, because it
was cloudy and I could not see below. To pass the hours—I was
really bored—I counted the number of times I chewed my airplane lunch.

It took 2,000 chews. On a later flight, this time from Tokyo
to New York nonstop, I was bored again, and decided to count
the chews involved in dinner, about 4,000. I was not awake
enough to count the number of times I chewed at breakfast, but
I'll throw in an arbitrary 1,000. That is 7,000 chews a day. This

concentration on an act we take for granted set about a whole chain reaction of thinking.

What happens when we chew? Each time, the softest tissue you can touch, the tip of your tongue, has to take food and roll it on both sides into the path of the hardest tissue you've got, your tooth enamel, and then get the hell out of the way before you bite.

Every now and then you bite your tongue and then you're sorry, but it's very rare. I haven't bitten mine in years. It's a very careful tongue—when I eat.

You are reading this book with the 120 million rods and cones in each of your two retinas. Those cones and rods have been installed in just the right way. You see these pages—you see creation—in 3-D. That is, each eye receives a different picture and your brain puts it together. Do you object? No, this is the space with which you see the world. This is the space between us.

If you looked at a diagram of the human ear, you would think that it's just too complicated to work. If you looked at a transparent model of a human being, and the intricate folds of nervous and circulatory systems, you'd say that they cannot possibly work, either.

My friend Alan Nixon, former president of the American Chemical Society, told me that the human body can carry out 100,000 different chemical reactions. Fortunately, you don't have to run your reactions or nervous or circulatory system. You don't have to worry about your ears, or whether your tongue will get out of the way when you bite. The food you had will be distributed to the trillions of cells in your body. The system goes on. If we had to think about it, we'd probably screw up.

I get a little excited talking about these things, what I call the wildness within. It's my "Gee whiz!" factor: *The whole immune system, incredible!* Of course, you're especially impressed if you've been kept more or less intact for eighty-two years.

We don't know how most of this is done, but our bodies do. What else has been passed along the genetic train that we haven't yet realized? Why do we have intuition? Intuition is quite important. It reminds you to be frightened when you may be too stunned to remember why.

These autopilot systems remind me of the colony of leaf-cutting ants in Professor E. O. Wilson's office at Harvard. Wilson likes ants, and probably knows more about them than anyone else. He showed me the colony at work. He put some leaves, which were about half the size of your hand, into a plastic box. The colony and the plastic food box were joined with a small branch. The ants cut the leaves into little pieces and brought them to their nest. Inside the nest they had a retinue of smaller ants that belonged to the same colony. The littler ants took the leaf pieces and cut them into smaller pieces. Then still smaller ants took them below to feed the fungi, which become the food they take to the young. This is one of the best examples of sustainable agriculture going. They also carry the ant poop to a greater depth, which enriches the soil.

Professor Wilson said, "Watch this," and rapped on the glass of the nest. Up from the chaos of debris came the warriors, three times the size of the larger workers, their mandibles capable of cutting leather. If I could understand ant language, I might have heard them ask, "What's wrong up here?" Finding nothing wrong, they went below to resume goofing off.

The weight of all the ants on the Earth happens to be greater than the weight of all of us. These little ants do not like clear-cutting, they don't use herbicides, they don't like our pesticides or chemical fertilizers. And informed by chemical signals from the queen, they know exactly what they're doing.

They are as well instructed as the arctic tern, a bird that migrates from pole to pole. The young of the arctic tern begin their long migration before the parents do, so you can see what good maps they are born with. It now occurs to me that the arctic tern isn't that good. If you start from the North Pole, south is the only direction there is, so how could you get lost? It's harder for the monarch butterfly. East of the Rockies, monarchs from Canada and the United States go to Mexico for the winter, to one little piece of forest, where the right trees are. West of the Rockies, they go to Pacific Grove, California. No parent guides them. Their genes carry flawless maps.

These are just a few of the miracles of wildness we're getting rid of without even knowing what we are eliminating. As Noel Brown, director of the United Nations Environment Programme, once put it, we may have already destroyed the cure for AIDS. How much of the pharmacological basis underlying modern medicine is rooted, literally, in forest plants, for instance? As Jay Hair of the National Wildlife Federation tells it, when his daughter was three, her doctor said, "She has four days to live." Today she is in graduate school. The medicine that cured her disease came from the rosy periwinkle, which grew only on the island of Madagascar and is now extinct.

We need to tire of trashing wildness. It's not making us happy. It's not making us healthy. It is making us miserable and despairing. Killing trees, habitat, and animals, and separating ourselves from nature is making us all a bit crazy. We need to restore the Earth because we need to save the wild. We need to save the wild in order to save ourselves.

AS HUMANS, we have the ability to feel compassion, to love, to reproduce, to think, to avoid annihilation. How did we acquire our wildness within? How did this magic come about?

The minimum genetic material required to build and operate all the human beings who have ever lived on Earth, about 100 billion of us, would fit into a sphere one-sixth of an inch in diameter. All the messages as to where the rods and cones should go, the development of our minds, conscious and unconscious, were developed over the last three and a half billion years, through trial and error, through success and failure, through symbiosis. We all still possess a little fragment of the first bit of life on Earth. Consequently, everything that's alive is related—and a submicroscopic part of us all is three and a half billion years old. Some of us show that age more than others.

But how did this miracle happen? What shaped it? It wasn't civilization because there wasn't any. It was something else. It was wilderness. Because that's all there was.

As Nancy Newhall said, wilderness is the ultimate encyclope-dia, holding the answers to questions that we have not yet learned how to ask. Yet with our technology, and for short-term jobs, or out of greedlock, or simply from not understanding what is hap-pening, we are obliterating what little wilderness we have left.

There have been many evolutionary failures. Millions upon millions of species are no longer here. Evolution did them in. But *we* are here, *you* are here.

So why should we insist on wiping out species a thousand times faster than evolution did—when that malpractice might easily wipe us out?

Every species that is lost diminishes our environment, the Earth. When we do this to ourselves, it degrades us and lessens our chance of there being a human future. There will be no joy in being almost ancestors.

If we are to restore our natural capital, then we must have examples of the true wild to work from. How shall we figure the future out, how shall we be able to help ourselves, if we find we have paved, logged, polluted, burned, and condominiumized the templates? Burning books is something most of us don't like to do. It worries us when it happens. We should be annoyed, like Thoreau a century and a half ago, at people who are playing demigod by tearing out the pages of the poem that is the Earth, and mutilating the best passages.

That poem contains us.

PART IV

Wildness

CHAPTER 16

Where the Wilderness Is

In wildness is the preservation of the world.

—Henry David Thoreau

IN WILDNESS is the preservation of the world. I liked
that line so much when I was executive director of the Sierra
Club that I used it for the title of a Thoreau anthology, illustrated
with photographs by Eliot Porter. The book, quite expensive, was
third in the club's exhibit-format series. If you just looked at the
floating autumn leaves on the cover and that title, "In Wildness Is
the Preservation of the World," you would get the message. My wife
said nobody would buy a book with such a title. So far, a million
people have.

When you lose contact with wildness, you've lost an important part of yourself. I think it makes people sad, without their
even knowing why, deep down. Wildness is also a fairly good
control of hubris. When you understand how recent an arrival
we are, in comparison with a forest or a mountain, and you begin

to understand how much wildness contributed to making us as a successful evolutionary project, you acquire some humility.

It is not hard to imagine a society that has lost its wilderness. Too much of Europe is such a place. China is such a place. Sometimes, I wonder if that loss leads to things like the Tiananmen Square massacre in 1989. Is it possible that our more arrogant tendencies run rampant, like scared rabbits, in the absence of wilderness?

A river like the North Fork of the Flathead, Tom McGuane wrote in 1994, "ought to go through South-Central Los Angeles" because of the calming effect it might have. That is a teasing thought. "The average American," McGuane continues, "is two-thirds river water and ought to have more sense about these things than he has shown. Obviously, a creature that is itself made mostly of rivers would do well to offer itself to the exaltation of rivers in good works and ceremonial acts of worship like fishing and contemplative floating in poetic watercraft such as canoes and jonboats."

Something called the Los Angeles River still runs in Los Angeles, but in a concrete channel and only now and then. It does not calm Los Angeles.

Neither Los Angeles nor a bonsai is a good substitute for wilderness.

THE GALÁPAGOS Islands contain wildness for which there is no substitute. Anne and I were delighted to discover that you could still walk among basking seals without their moving away, or among frigate birds, and that birds saw fit to land on us. Certainly, I never expected to be courted by a blue-footed booby, and briefly thought I was until I moved myself out of her way so she could court a creature bluer footed than I.

Nevertheless, I concluded that our own major wilderness areas in North America are wilder than anything in the Galápagos, although our wildlife will never be as untroubled by people. Our wilderness will remain wilder so long as we stop chopping away at it. That said, let's remember that only about 4 percent of the United States is designated wilderness, and half of this is in Alaska. Loopholes abound in the legal language protecting these remnants, and each generation must review the gems left it by the generation before, and be ready to guard the house against burglars. The well-traveled Sierra and the lonely Bob Marshall Wilderness in Montana, according to an army study for World War II, are the only two places in the Lower Forty-eight where you can get more than ten miles away from a road.

But what exquisite places.

Bob Marshall—he hated to be called anything but plain Bob—was the wild conscience of the second Roosevelt Administration. We have a wilderness system in America in large part because of Bob, who once wrote a reply to a woman who insisted on calling him Mr. Marshall: "When you call me Mr. Marshall it makes me feel so thoroughly miserable I want to knock head against the side of a house." I met him only once always admired his uncompromising stance. He wrote but "one hope of repulsing the tyrannical ambition of to conquer every niche on the whole Earth. That hope is the organization of spirited people who will fight for the freedom of wilderness."

Bob formed the Wilderness Society with Aldo Leopold and others, such as Benton MacKaye. They are great Americans, great citizens of the Earth, and should be recognized as such, along with Howard Zahniser, who wrote the definition of wilderness that is now the law: "A wilderness, in contrast with those areas where man and his own works dominate the landscape, is hereby recognized as an area where the Earth and its community of life are untrammeled by man, where man himself is a visitor who does not remain."

To me, a wilderness is where the flow of wildness is essentially uninterrupted by technology; without wilderness, the world's a cage. To Mrs. Malaprop, it is where the hand of man has not set foot. To Bob Marshall, if you set foot in it, you shouldn't be able to cross it unless you sleep out. It would have to be that big. Take your choice, and remember that there is no better place to rediscover the wildness the ages have made perfect—and beyond that, there are still stars out there to make the night friendly. When did you last see the stars?

Aldo Leopold was one of the first to counsel, "Think like a mountain." He wrote: "Man always kills the thing he loves, and we the pioneers have killed our wilderness. Some say we had Be that as it may, I am glad I shall never be young without country to be young in. Of what avail are forty freedoms t a blank spot on the map?"

CHAPTER 17

Listening to Mountains

Flocks of birds have flown high and away.
A solitary drift of cloud, too, has gone, wandering on.
And I sit alone with the Ching-Ting Peak, towering beyond.
We never grow tired of each other, the mountain and I.

—Li Po

I CLIMBED many mountains between 1930 and 1956, and I keep climbing them in my dreams. I have never considered it to be a victory to stand alone or with my companions on the mountaintop. That is not the right way to view what has happened after a successful ascent. The mountain merely relaxed for a moment. I didn't beat the mountain, but I did earn it.

The thrill of helicoptering up to virgin powder in order to ski trackless snow has spread from Aspen to Alaska. But it seems to me that it takes the earning out of skiing. I believe in cross-country skis, not snowmobiles. I hate to see the challenge diminished.

What you've earned, you are glad you've got. You put part of yourself into getting it. It is not spoon-fed. And people who believe there are getting to be too many restrictions in wilderness areas need to get out and organize for more wilderness.

We certainly need it. When I climbed Shiprock in 1937, when I earlier made the attempt on Mount Waddington in 1935, there were fewer than 1,000 climbers in the country. Now we have about 250,000. Today we have indoor climbing gymnasiums, and outside we are beginning to damage the mountains themselves. I did it myself, with those pitons and expansion bolts I used on Shiprock.

Today there are something like 6,000 or 7,000 expansion bolt holes in Yosemite Valley alone. This worries me. Some of the perpetrators say that their expansion bolts are only used for safety. If so, fine. But if they are being used for ego, not safety, that is another thing entirely.

"Ego bolts" are employed in order to find a new way up a cliff that could not otherwise be climbed. Climbers sometimes put in the bolts with a battery-powered portable drill as they rappel, then they use the bolts to make the ascent. I think this demeans mountaineering.

It's like anything else. As long as you think there is an unlimited supply of something, then you think it will replace itself, if you think at all.

When I was climbing, there were so few people yet so many cliffs. We didn't think we could ever bother those cliffs. When we came upon a crack on the mountain that had vegetation, we would dig it out. We called this gardening. When you climb a tough mountain, you want to stand on solid rock, not on a flower or on moss. We would just toss the garden over the edge.

Today there aren't so many alpine gardens left. Today we've also got the white cliffs of Yosemite, because so many people are assiduously chalking hands to make them hold better.

If young climbers need to do these things for protection, and don't damage the mountain, OK. But if they cannot make the top without damaging the mountain, then I say, try something else. Skydiving. Windsurfing. Hang gliding. Ping-Pong. Let the mountain be.

LOREN EISELEY suggested that rocks and mountains just move more slowly than we do, so slowly that we can't understand their motion very well. Loren explained more than mountains to me in person and in books. He wrote, "We are compounded of dust and the light of a star." What power in so few words!

François Matthes provided scientific detail. He talked about the tracks that rocks will leave on a slope. Imagine a slope. The sun rises. The rock warms, expands, and moves infinitesimally upward, perpendicular to the slope. The sun sets. The rock cools, and moves infinitesimally but vertically down, with gravity. That works out to be a daily tiny triangle. The track it leaves can be measured in the lichen. It takes a long time for the lichen to grow back, maybe fifty or a hundred years. Slowly, you see, the rock makes its mark. Of course, some rocks move faster, like the big block I pulled out climbing the Thumb in the Sierra in 1933. Miraculously, I avoided falling with it.

I believe that mountains should accept natural deterioration, because that's in their destiny. But I don't think we should mess them up. We've messed up enough things, besides mountains, to last us for several more civilizations. There are better sports than that.

LET THE MOUNTAINS talk. The mountains first talked to me through poets I had to read in junior high English. Longfellow first:

> This is the forest primeval.
> The murmuring pines and the hemlocks,
> Bearded with moss, and in garments green, indistinct
> in the twilight,
> Stand like Druids of eld, with voices sad and prophetic. . . .

I could hear what was happening in Sir Walter Scott's lead to *The Lady of the Lake*:

> The stag at eve had drunk his fill,
> Where danced the moon on Monan's rill,
> And deep his midnight lair had made
> In lone Glenartney's hazel shade.

Thoreau came much later, when in *Walden* he told how to get where you can hear mountains talk:

Rise free from care before the dawn and seek adventures. Let the noon find you by other lakes and the night overtake thee everywhere at home. . . . Let the thunder rumble. . . .

Soon I would hear the talk directly. Not too sonorously from the thunder, cascading water, or falling stone, but musically enough from the jay's complaint, the kookaburra's laugh, the coyote's howl, pines answering the wind, fallen leaves answering your shuffling feet, and the lilting notes of a stream, hermit thrush, or canyon wren completing the symphony.

Twelve centuries earlier, Li Po wrote of what I can hear with my spirit:

Flocks of birds have flown high and away.
A solitary drift of cloud, too, has gone, wandering on.
And I sit alone with the Ching-Ting Peak, towering beyond.
We never grow tired of each other, the mountain and I.

I believe we should listen eloquently. Try still harder and you may find that all your senses can talk to you. You handicap yourself if you don't let them.

Not everybody is able to climb real mountains, of course, whether or not they try hard. That probably must apply to me.

For all its benefits, age can get in the way. How much access should be provided handicapped people—handicapped in the normal sense? I am thinking of a discussion we had when Franklin Roosevelt came to see the new national park, Kings Canyon, that he had helped us establish in the Sierra. Because of polio, he had to be lifted into his car. San Joaquin Valley officials wanted to construct a road into the new park so that he could be driven in. Will Colby, who was serving his half a century as Sierra Club secretary, said, "If we don't have that road, President Roosevelt won't be able to see the canyon."

We shouldn't have built that road, even for the president, but the commitment had been made. The road was built, though it was kept very short. I agree there should be a good sampling of things for handicapped people to experience. But if you make it easy for anybody to get into wilderness, it isn't wilderness any longer. Don't do it for me. I don't want it to be any easier for me to get to that place in Yosemite that is informally called Browers' Bench—if I want to go again, I'll simply have to get back in shape, or crawl.

I HAVEN'T DONE any serious climbing since 1956. The serious part that year was my decision to stop at the *bergschrund*, the highest crevasse on the glacier under the north face of the Grand Teton. I was older than my companions by thirteen and twenty-four years, respectively, and I didn't see why my handicap of age should be shared. So Dick Emerson, who became the outstanding mountaineer-ranger in the Tetons, and Phil Berry, who would twice be president of the Sierra Club, made the ascent. I learned to share the attitude expressed when Benton MacKaye told me, in his eighties, "I don't have to climb Katahdin anymore." Mount Katahdin, in Maine, is where the sun first hits the continental United States.

Like many somewhat older people who have enjoyed many somewhat strenuous sports, I had no thoughts that my mountaineering, that is, my difficult mountaineering, would end. Three years ago I was in Florence, Italy, at a meeting of world-class climbers, who had invited me anyway. The group included a young man who had climbed the Eigerwand solo, in winter. Unbelievable! And there, in a slide show, was eighty-six-year-old Fritz Wiesner, doing a 5.11 (a harder climb, on the mountaineers' scale, than I would like to dream of climbing).

That shook me. I announced that I was going home to Berkeley, getting in shape, getting the right shoes, and getting back on a rock. Well, I got back to Berkeley, but so far I haven't even got the right shoes.

CHAPTER 18

Rachel Carson's Pelicans

The pelican remembers the cone from which the first
redwood fell.

—Robinson Jeffers

A LITTLE WHILE ago, I was counting brown pelicans
and remembering Rachel Carson.

I was sitting in Sinbad's Restaurant on the San Francisco wa-
terfront, as I have off and on for twenty years, waiting patiently
for my poached salmon to arrive. The pelicans were putting on a
show as they glided under the Bay Bridge, then dropped to coast
low and long on their bow waves. Sometimes from my table at
Sinbad's I count five or six pelicans, sometimes many more. My
record for one day is 176, which includes lunch and happy hour.
Pelicans are among the biggest birds in North America, the
brown a little smaller than the white, which has a ten-foot wing-
spread. My empathy is with the browns, the ones almost put out
of business by DDT.

No one likes pelicans better than I do. Rachel Carson also liked pelicans, and did a great deal to save them, beginning with her book, *Silent Spring*, in 1962, which awakened the world and shook me, too. Rachel explained how DDT weakened the shells of pelicans' eggs, and the eggs of many other birds. Spring in America was becoming as silent as winter. Barely measurable amounts of insecticide could impair cell functions, such as reproduction. Rachel made it clear that living cells, whether in birds, insects, or humans, had important elements in common. What we did to end a function in insects could have a boomerang effect we might not like. That truth has not sunk in far enough yet. We may discover that industry is giving us a quicker life through chemistry—and it will take chemists to save us.

In the late 1960s, my family and I visited Eliot Porter on his family's island, Great Spruce Head, in Penobscot Bay, Maine. On an islet in a channel was a tree with a nest. Sitting on the nest was a female osprey. Around the island were other trees with nests abandoned by ospreys who could not make their DDT-damaged eggs hatch. Flying in from the water came the male osprey. As we watched, he hovered, and the female flew off the nest to join him in midair. They seemed almost to confer. Then they just went away together, abandoning that nest and the hopeless eggs. It just wasn't working. DDT had ended the life in them. Anne and I shared the ospreys' grief.

Rachel's book led to the banning of DDT, at least in the United States, but banning has not reduced its persistence, and unscrupulous chemical companies still manufacture the compound elsewhere, inhibiting restoration and who knows what else.

PELICANS AND Rachel Carson are linked, for me, and I remember the last time I saw her. She asked me to help her see the redwoods in Muir Woods. Anne and our daughter, Barbara, became the friendly native guides, joined by a National Park Service guide, with a wheelchair for Rachel. She had come to California for a conference. Terminal cancer could not prevent her from working.

From Muir Woods we drove to the shore at Fort Cronkhite, now part of the Golden Gate National Recreation Area. In the lagoon just inland were perhaps fifty brown pelicans having a hell of a good time, perhaps celebrating the beginning of their recovery with a pelican ballet, on that sunny day. I have to believe in magic, for what else could have led those pelicans to know that Rachel Carson would have preferred them to redwoods?

I DON'T KNOW how much money the chemical industry invested in trying and failing to discredit Rachel Carson. It must be proprietary information. So far, we hear, they are putting up $15 million to discredit Theo Colburn, the Rachel Carson reincarnate, and her associates, who are coming up with a most alarming message about the silent toxic sea of artificial estrogens polluting our water as DDT once did the land. Chemistry, in the natural process of our evolution, is self-controlling. In less experienced hands, it is producing uncounted, perhaps uncountable, products nature cannot handle, nor can we.

The things Rachel warned about more than thirty years ago reformed the environmental movement, but the public is forgetting. What the chemical industry is now trying to silence, we are forced to infer, is Theo Colburn's new message—the chemical assault on the male. Especially the human male. This half of humanity, which is still running most of the chemical industry (and government), is likely to become effectively concerned about what certain chemicals, odorless, colorless, and tasteless but not timeless, can do to the sperm and its distribution system— especially when we apply these chemicals without knowing what we are doing or how many generations it will affect. Like the human egg, the sperm knows the facts of life and shouldn't be decimated, or worse, have two heads and no tail.

So if you see chemical industry ads and articles by indentured scientists that say everything is OK, prepare to accept them the same way you accept the tobacco industry's assurances that smoking, first- and secondhand, is no problem.

Listen carefully to Theo. Remember Rachel.

WHILE THE PELICANS outside Sinbad's glided past, I also thought about condors. The salmon and hollandaise were trying to get together in the kitchen, and Chardonnay was my solace. In that

morning's paper, July 7, 1994, I had read a short article from the
Associated Press:

California Condor Back in Captivity

A California condor in Los Angeles has been returned to
captivity because it did not adapt to life in the wild. The
male condor, hatched in a zoo program to rebuild the
wild population of the endangered birds, was one of two
who flew back to civilization. He was captured Monday.

A condor is about 5 percent feathers, blood, and bone, and
about 95 percent place. Place designs the condor, as it does the
arctic tern and the monarch butterfly. A condor must learn to
know the wind, where to find food and water, where to nest,
where to hang out. A young condor remains at the nest for a year,
and accompanies its parents for another five, a little like a human
child—but how the condor can fly!

I was seventy-two before I saw my first condor, and what an
extraordinary creature it was! Stable as a 747, feathering the wind
with just the tips of its primaries, soaring and rising higher and
higher on a convenient thermal, then gliding on and on and on
and out of sight without flapping a wing. How lazy can you get?

Thirty years ago, there was a big argument, of which I was a
part, of how best to save the condor. Take it out of the wild and
raise it in a captive breeding program, or leave it where it is and
protect its habitat. With the condor, I said, if you want to save

the species, you must save the place. That may not be true for all birds, but that is the law for the condor.

We lost the argument. The biologists wanted an interesting and well-funded program they would get to manage. The Audubon Society thought it might work. The owners of the large tracts of coastal Californian land that comprised the condors' habitat wanted to develop their lands. I could understand that last part. Who was going to compensate the owners for the loss of their lands, just because condors had always lived there?

Today people still push captive-breeding programs instead of habitat protection. Sometimes captive-breeding works. Other times it is a device for getting a creature out of the way.

When my salmon finally arrived before me at Sinbad's, I had mixed emotions. I was glad to see lunch. I missed Rachel Carson. I missed the condors. And I was glad the pelicans would be back, same time, same place, but different and abundant, another day.

CHAPTER 19

Neat Tricks

IT IS FUN to discover how nature works, to find
out, for example, that humans have to make cement at 1,800
degrees Fahrenheit, while a hen can make stronger cement at 103
degrees, and a clam can do still better at the temperature of sea-
water. What's the trick? We still don't know. If we found out,
would we pave everything in sight?

Other neat tricks: The bombardier beetle produces actual
steam in an internal chamber and fires it at its enemies. Another
beetle modifies the surface tension of water with a detergent that
sinks water skaters for an easy meal. Another beetle can inject a
frog with a chemical that liquefies everything inside the frog's
skin, and then has a drink. (The U.S. Department of Defense
should not be told about this until it firmly commits to restoration.)

There's all this exciting stuff! We haven't spoiled it all, and have only begun to learn about it. With vision, we can spare what's left.

Allow me to offer you a short course in ecology, beginning with rot. Rot is an extraordinarily important process. Rot is highly exciting. But we give it a three-letter word. We say, "This tree is sick," and "This is rotten, anyway. We should get rid of it."

By removing the rotten tree from the forest, we knock out of existence all the species that were going to use that tree for a home, for their dinner, until it rotted away completely, and helped to nourish the next tree, maybe 200 or more years down the line. This is a very good system. Unfortunately, we've learned to interrupt it rather than to live with it. We have learned how to break the circle of life instead of respecting it.

Nature recycles everything. There isn't anything that isn't recycled. Go outside. Look at the natural systems. Study them and learn to read the Earth. You will see what it has had time to learn. You will begin to understand the life force.

"The cold smokeless fires of decay"—which are what rot is—require energy. I may be wrong in this, but I believe there's a little surplus everywhere in nature. We may live on some of that surplus, but we must not take so much that we destroy the system.

My apple tree will produce a whole bunch of apples, and if I don't mistreat it, it will probably last far longer than I will. Apple trees live almost 100 years. I'll use some while I can, but none will be unused. All that time, those half-eaten apples that the squirrels let fall to the ground will feed other species. There are far more apples than the apple tree needed just to reproduce itself, or for me to make applesauce from.

Part of the recycling of nature is to make sure that the other forms of life that are necessary to their own recycling circles are fed along the way. Life is a circle of nourishment. Some might call it inefficient, but they would be wrong. The natural law, hard to explain, is that efficiency and stability are incompatible.

What is a tree really up to? What is a tree about? It locks up carbon. If that carbon gets buried by floods and mud, and begins to collect downstream, it begins to form the beginnings of the fossil fuel inventory available for whatever, or to whomever, centuries from now. That's recycling. The carbon is taken out of the system for a while.

That is only part of what is happening. Most of this change takes place above ground. While it is alive, the tree frees oxygen as well as locking up carbon. While all this green stuff is living on the surface of the Earth, we have the oxygen that it has made free. This is rather important for us, if we like breathing. That's why I have been saying that we have a large potential constituency, as environmentalists: those who like breathing. Or those who wish their great-grandchildren might breathe at all.

When we burn carbon for energy, we free carbon monoxide and dioxide. If we burn too much, we've got problems. Carbon monoxide kills, and we may well overload the carbon dioxide sink. That can change the fate of the biosphere, the fate of the Earth, us. This is called the greenhouse effect.

It does not have to be this way.

One-third of the energy that comes from the sun is reflected back to outer space, beyond our jurisdiction so far. Another third lifts water. It's a very nice system because it just lifts the good water. It leaves the salt and other ingredients behind. It was not nature's idea to put some things in the air to mix up with her clean water. These things dirty up the air, and acid rain develops. That was our idea, except for a volcano or two. Nature's idea was to lift up water and form clean raindrops and snowflakes.

Snow stores water very nicely. Are we trying to get rid of that benefit by bringing up the temperature of the Earth so that we no longer get snow? Snow is a fairly important form of water storage.

Then we realize that, to serve ourselves, we need to intercept that water. Some people who consider themselves really bright human beings consider that any water that flows to the sea is wasted. I believe that to be wasted thinking.

The unintercepted water that comes from the land brings nutrients and minerals that are terribly important for everything that lives in the ocean. We keep trying to interrupt that flow, through dams and diversions, and by dumping in things that nature can't handle.

The commercials on television tell you the oven cleaner will just clean your oven. You spray the chemical on and everything you don't like disappears. But it doesn't disappear when you flush it down the drain. It moves toward the ocean and it kills. What systems does it destroy that ultimately are used to build our own bodies? The Earth knows how to recycle mountains safely. It may gag on oven cleaner. Oven cleaner removes grease, and may ultimately remove you.

Enjoy watching nature at work. The sun lifts the water. The water washes the mountains down. Then the tectonic plates say, "Oh, no, you don't!" and push the mountains back up. That's long-term recycling. Water is very good at taking mountains apart. If it weren't for the tectonic plates, the world would be flat by now. So be grateful for tectonic plates. Keep them moving! Except if you live in Los Angeles.

PART V

Saving the Earth

CHAPTER 20

The Third Planet:
Operating Instructions

TECTONIC PLATES are maintenance-free, or are they?

Let the Mountains Talk was written for Earth Day 1995, the twenty-fifth anniversary of Earth Day. Twenty years earlier I wrote an endpaper for the *New York Times Magazine*, with the title, "The Third Planet: Operating Instructions." The *Reader's Digest* reprinted the endpaper, and then it became a booklet. More than 18 million copies got around. But I am a little worried we've misplaced the instructions again. They need restoring. Here they are, for a new generation and a new Earth Day.

THIS PLANET *has been delivered wholly assembled and in perfect working condition, and is intended far fully automatic and trouble-free operation in orbit around its star, the Sun.*

However, to insure proper functioning, all passengers are requested to familiarize themselves fully with the following instructions. Loss or even temporary misplacement of these instructions may result in calamity. Passengers who must proceed without the benefit of these rules are likely to cause considerable damage before they can learn the proper operating procedures for themselves.

Components

It is recommended that passengers become completely familiar with the following planetary components:

1. *Air.* The air accompanying this planet is not replaceable. Enough has been supplied to cover the land and the water, but not very deeply. In fact, if the atmosphere were reduced to the density of water, then it would be a mere 33 feet deep. In normal use, the air is self-cleaning. It may be cleaned in part if excessively soiled. The passengers' lungs will be of help—up to a point. However, they will discover that anything they throw, spew, or dump into the air will return to them in due course. Since passengers will need to use the air, on the average, every five seconds, they should treat it accordingly.

2. *Water.* The water supplied with this planet isn't replaceable either. The operating water supply is very limited: if the Earth were the size of an egg, all the water on it would fit into a single drop. The water contains many creatures, almost all of which eat and may be eaten; these creatures may be eaten by

human passengers. If disagreeable things are dispersed in the planet's water, however, caution should be observed, since the water creatures concentrate the disagreeable things in their tissues. If human passengers eat the water creatures, they will add disagreeable things to their diet. In general, passengers are advised not to disdain water, which is what they mostly are.

3. *Land.* Although the surface of the planet is varied and seems abundant, only a small amount of land is suited to growing things, and that essential part should not be misused. It is also recommended that no attempt be made to disassemble the surface too deeply inasmuch as the land is supported by a molten and very hot underlying layer that will grow little but volcanoes.

4. *Life.* The foregoing components help make life possible. There is only one life per passenger, and it should be treated with dignity. Instructions covering the birth, operation and maintenance, and disposal for each living entity have been thoughtfully provided. These instructions are contained in a complex language, called the DNA code, which is not easily understood. However, this does not matter, as the instructions are fully automatic. Passengers are cautioned, however, that radiation and many dangerous chemicals can damage the instructions severely. If in any way living species are destroyed, or rendered unable to reproduce, the filling of reorders is subject to long delays.

5. *Fire.* This planet has been designed and fully tested at the factory for totally safe operation with fuel constantly transmitted from a remote source, the Sun, provided at absolutely no charge.

The following must be observed with greatest care: The planet comes with a limited reserve fuel supply, contained in fossil deposits, which should be used only in emergencies. Use of this reserve fuel supply entails hazards, including the release of certain toxic metals, which must be kept out of the air and the food supply of living things. The risk will not be appreciable if the use of the emergency fuel is extended over the operating life of the planet. Rapid use, if sustained only for a brief period, may produce unfortunate results.

Maintenance

The kinds of maintenance will depend upon the number and constituency of the passengers. If only a few million human passengers wish to travel at a given time, no maintenance will be required, and no reservations will be necessary. The planet is self-maintaining, and the external fuel source will provide exactly as much energy as is needed or can be safely used. However, if a very large number of people insist on boarding at one time, serious problems will result, requiring costly solutions.

Operation

Barring extraordinary circumstances, it is necessary only to observe the mechanism periodically and to report any irregularities to the Smithsonian Institution. However, if owing to misuse of the planet's mechanism, observations show a substantial change in the predictable patterns of sunrise and sunset, passengers should prepare to leave the vehicle.

Emergency Repairs

If, through no responsibility of the current passengers, damage to the planet's operating mechanisms has been caused by ignorant or careless action of the previous travelers, it is best to request the Manufacturer's assistance (best obtained through prayer).

Upon close examination, this planet will be found to consist of complex and fascinating detail in design and structure. Some passengers, upon discovering these details in the past, have attempted to replicate or improve the design and structure, or have even claimed to have invented them. The Manufacturer, having among other things invented the opposable thumb, may be amused by this. It is reliably reported that at this point, however, it appears to the Manufacturer that a full panoply of consequences of this thumb idea will not be without an element of unwelcome surprise.

CHAPTER 21

Unwise Misuse

> As we lengthen and elaborate the chain of technology that
> intervenes between us and the natural world, we forget that
> we become steadily more vulnerable to even the slightest
> failure in that chain.
>
> —Paul B. Sears

WHEN MAURICE STRONG became the first head of the
United Nations Environment Programme, he told the following story:

A fire broke out in a crowded theater. Everybody rose up
and started for the exits. But the piano player, sensing the
impending panic, promptly began to play the piano. He
played so well, and with such nonchalance and assurance,
that the audience returned to their seats—and burned to
death.

Rush Limbaugh, the most popular critic of the environmental movement, plays the piano in his best-seller *The Way Things
Ought to Be*:

Mount Pinatubo in the Philippines spewed forth more than a thousand times the amount of ozone-depleting chemicals in one eruption than all the fluorocarbons manufactured by wicked, diabolical, and insensitive corporations in history. . . . Mankind can't possibly equal the output of even one eruption from Pinatubo, much less 4 billion years' worth of them, so how can we destroy the ozone?

Mr. Limbaugh considers those who worry about ozone and other environmental concerns to be "dunderheaded alarmists and prophets of doom" and "environmental wackos." On the late-night American news show "Nightline," Mr. Limbaugh, who was debating then-Senator Al Gore, said, "Mount Pinatubo has put 570 times the amount of chlorine into the atmosphere in one eruption than all the man-made chlorofluorocarbons in one year"—forgetting that chlorine and CFCs are different animals.

Although I think Mr. Limbaugh's numbers need to be carefully checked at all times, I'll just settle for simple logic. It is not given to us to control volcanoes or errant asteroids, ice ages, the arrival and departure of the atmosphere, or the frequency of big bangs. We can, and ought to, control our own excesses. I have come to like the ozone barrier. Why add to its troubles?

Mr. Limbaugh also tends to think loosely about the number of trees chopped down in our forests, about the dangers of dioxin, and about any number of other environmental concerns, long documented and accepted by scientists.

He reminds me of a less charming lad who was put out of business in the 1950s, Senator Joe McCarthy. It was not a questioning of his abuse of the facts that shamed Senator McCarthy before his formerly adoring public, but rather a simple question put to him by Joseph Welch, the attorney for the U.S. Army: "Have you no sense of decency, Sir, at long last?"

He obviously did not, and that was it. Enough was enough. "You can't fool all the people for very long."

If Mr. Limbaugh, and people like him, were to debate me, I would be tempted to repeat Welch's query or ask something like "Do you believe in compunction?" or "Are you serious?" However, as I have grown older, I have mellowed a bit. I am sometimes more curious than angry, so I would also want to ask: "How did you reach your present conclusions?" I'd listen and try to explain how I reached mine. I'd hope to persuade him that, as usual, I was right and he wasn't. And I'd try not to forget tact and resort to asking how he ever developed such a mean mouth. How did he ever come to choose Dixy Lee Ray as his expert? We have 2,000 scientists and 100 Nobel laureates who disagree with her "science." And did he ever wonder how much he and she cost the Earth?

The reason he has such a big audience is that his fans would rather feel comfortable than feel alarmed. If they feel comfortable enough, they see no reason to change their ways. But I'll bet that if you become alarmed at all the real dangers to the land, to the sources of our clean water, to the atmosphere, to the species that are disappearing, your natural inclination would probably not be to do what he does. I believe you would—and he should—think it better to get off the track before the locomotive wants your space.

You could say that the old Reagan-Bush leaguers are in it for the billions, that for all their red-white-and-blue chest pounding, they have been shills for transnational corporations. I believe Limbaugh to be sincere, but sincerely wrong.

But then there's the so-called Wise Use Movement, or as National Park Service Director Roger Kennedy calls it, "the Unwise Misuse Movement." The Wise Use mission seems to be to weaken the Endangered Species Acts, allow oil and gas development and mining in national parks and designated wilderness, and make sure anyone can travel to any part of the wilderness they want with the aid of an internal-combustion engine such as snowmobile, off-road vehicle, or dirt bike. Wise Users also have a *Me first!* idea of traditional property rights. These folks are tough. They are well funded. Fortunately, they lack grassroots members. Enough people in America understand the need for wilderness.

Here are some of the principal recent donors to the People for the West!, a Wise Use group, as reported by *Audubon* magazine:

Nerco Minerals Co., $100,000
Cyprus Minerals, $100,000
Chevron USA, $45,000

Home Stake Mining Co., $15,000

Energy Fuels, $15,000

Hecla Mining Co., $30,000

Bond Gold Corp., $30,000

Pegasus Gold Corp., $15,000

I think it only natural that Chevron USA would see fit to donate $45,000 to People for the West!, since one of the organization's other missions has been to uphold the antiquated 1872 mining law governing hard-rock mining. That law let Chevron buy the 2,036 acres that make up the Stillwater mine, which sits forty miles over the Beartooth-Absaroka Wilderness from Yellowstone Park, for a total of only $10,180. That, according to the Mineral Policy Center, amounts to $5 an acre. A good deal, considering that the mine, with its reserves of palladium and platinum, is worth an estimated $30 billion.

I have nothing against making a profit. You must have accumulation from one thing in order to accomplish something else. Investments must come from somewhere. I am not going to attack the dollar. It's having a hard enough time on its own. If making some money is going to encourage people to do things, fine, but I want their profit to lead them on to do good and better things. What concerns me is the impact of avarice on the Earth.

"These Wise Use extremists claim that economically you're going to take their jobs away from them; they're all going to become poor; their children are going to starve; and it's all because you're a bunch of fuzzy-headed tree huggers. . . . It's blatant lying in many cases in how they present things. . . ." This, from Gen. Norman Schwarzkopf, not usually known for his environmental radicalism. He was speaking at a press conference for the Nature Conservancy, a nongovernmental group that buys up sensitive land of notable ecological worth in order to preserve it.

Developers are entitled to just compensation when the public decides the lands they were to develop might better be put to use as, say, wilderness, rather than, say, to be clearcut for junk journals or developed into yet another ski resort. (And I have skied much of my life, as soldier and civilian.) But I do not believe a developer or timber owner should be compensated for the opportunity they may have lost. They should get what they paid out plus reasonable interest.

Otherwise, you create the opportunity for blackmailing the public. All over the West are lands left over from the checkerboard pattern of public and private ownership begun when Congress gave alternating sections to the railroads to encourage them to cross the country as quickly as possible. (Remember? They used to carry people on trains.) These parcels are sometimes in the middle of wilderness or adjoining it. Naturally, the public would like the owners not to clearcut the lands, and that desire can sometimes be manipulated, so that much more than fair market value is paid. Of course, many owners of forestlands want to do the right thing, at a fair price.

I am well aware that the Fifth Amendment to the U.S. Constitution reads, in part: "No person shall . . . be deprived of life, liberty, or property, without due process of law; nor shall private property be taken for public use without just compensation."

I believe Thomas Jefferson and James Madison had a bit of a hand in the writing of that Constitution. Here is an excerpt from a letter Jefferson wrote to Madison: "The Earth belongs in use to the living . . . no man can by natural right oblige the lands he occupies, or the persons who succeed him in that occupation, to the payment of debts contracted by him. For if he could, he might during his own life, eat up the use of the lands for several generations to come . . . then the Earth would belong to the dead and not the living generation. . . . No generation can contract debts greater than may be paid during the course of its own existence."

Wise use.

CHAPTER 22

Rule Number 6 Revisited

IT'S BEEN A WHILE since I have mentioned Rule
Number 6. If you've forgotten, Rule Number 6 is: Never take
yourself too seriously. This time it will be necessary to take a cir-
cuitous route to reach the rule, almost like flogging a dead horse,
as you will see.

One time, Howard Zahniser, whose patience and boldness as
head of The Wilderness Society were the main reasons for this
country's having a wilderness system, was addressing a wilderness
conference convened by the Federation of Western Outdoors
Clubs, and he began his address with an account of how he, Joe
Penfold, and I happened to carry a dead horse into a house in
Washington, D.C.

We three were walking from Zahnie's office to dinner at the Cosmos Club. Halfway down the block from P Street to Massachusetts Avenue, we came upon the dead horse. It was not a huge workhorse, but it was not a small horse, either.

A distraught man standing beside the horse begged us to help him carry the animal up the stairs into his house, which was right there.

It was no easy task. Zahnie, whose heart condition would lead to his death just before the Wilderness Bill was signed into law by President Johnson, could not apply as much energy as he would have liked to. He portaged the horse's head end up the stairs, Joe and I the other end. You can imagine with what difficulty we pushed and shoved that dead horse into the living room. Then the man asked us to help get the horse into the bathroom and put it in the bathtub.

Once you get involved in a situation like this, it is difficult to back out. It was a tight fit, but we got the horse into the bathtub.

We finally felt that we were due at least an explanation.

"Why, for the love of the Lord, did you ask us to do this?" asked Zahnie. Of course, anyone with due intelligence would have asked the question sooner, but Zahnie put tact first.

"Well," said the man, "it's this way. I share this house with a good friend. He is out of town for the weekend, but he will be home tonight. He's a good man, and for the most part we get along well. But he is constantly doing something that at first only

bothered me, but as time went by, really got to me. Almost in-variably, whenever I tell him something I've learned or think might interest him, he says, 'I know.' Whatever it is, he says, 'I know,' or 'Yeah, I know.'

"So he's coming home tonight, and I'm going to be sitting in the living room reading, and because it's been a long trip, the first thing he is going to do is go to the bathroom. Then he is going to charge out of the bathroom and say: 'There's a dead horse in the bathtub!'

"And I'm going to smile and say, 'I know.'"

The only problem with this story, which I happen to like, is that not a word of it is true, save for the fact that Zahnie was tact-ful. He did indeed tell the story to the wilderness conference as a shaggy-dog icebreaker.

Now there is a recent book with the title *Environmental Overkill*, by Dixy Lee Ray, who was once the governor of Wash-ington and chairman (her word) of the Atomic Energy Commis-sion. On page 204 she ascribes this quote to me: "While the death of young men in war is unfortunate, it is no more serious than the touching of mountains and wilderness areas by hu-mankind." This quote has many problems, but it does share one thing with Zahnie's tale: it is not true. It is made up. I lost too many good friends in World War II to have had such a compari-son ever cross my mind.

In the very next paragraph, Ms. Ray recounts how I told a travel group in Whistler, British Columbia: "Loggers losing their

jobs because of Spotted Owl legislation is, in my eyes, no different than people being out of work after the furnaces of Dachau shut down."

This, too, is a strong thing to say. I did not say it. Dick Cavett did—almost, but not quite.

Here's how a certain passage reads in my autobiography, For Earth's Sake: "How much sympathy should go to an industry that won't change its ways or workers who won't change theirs, until something has been destroyed that belongs to all the future, and not really to them?"

In environmental controversies, industry invariably brings up the question of jobs. So did Dick Cavett. When John McPhee's Encounters with the Archdruid was published, he asked the author to appear on his show. McPhee, with perhaps more modesty than was necessary, declined. As one might expect, the archdruid leapt at the opportunity, and was joined there by Arthur Godfrey. Mr. Cavett asked if I was alarmed by what was happening to the environment. Trying hard to sound reasonable, I gave a nondescript answer. Arthur Godfrey intervened to say, "It scares the hell out of me!"

Dick Cavett happened to look down at Mr. Godfrey's shoes, and could not forgo a comment about their being made of alligator leather. Then he went after me. "What," he asked, "do you tell those who say environmentalists are putting people out of work?"

I was about to come up with a nonconfrontational answer, but he didn't wait.

"I think I can answer that one," he said. "I suppose a lot of people lost their jobs when they closed the furnaces at Dachau."

Shocked by his own extemporaneity, he quickly changed the subject.

On the front cover of *Environmental Overkill* is a blurb from Rush Limbaugh. He says, "A way must be found to get this book into the hands of as many Americans as possible."

I wonder why?

WAIT, YOU SAY, what about Rule Number 6? Wasn't that the point? Rule Number 6 said not to take yourself so seriously. Sometimes it is hard. But you're right to insist. So I leave you with this:

Anne and I attended a party at an old friend's house not too long ago, and wandered into the kitchen. On top of the refrigerator was an unusual object. I remembered it later as an elephant's foot. She remembered it as the head of a hippopotamus. We argued about it and could not agree. We did agree that our hostess was Barbara Bedayn. To end the argument, I asked Anne to call Barbara, which she did.

"Is this Barbara?"

"Yes."

"Are you in the kitchen?"

"Yes."

"On top of the refrigerator, is that an elephant's foot or the head of a hippopotamus?"

There was a silent pause, then the answer—and all of this is true:

"Honey, I think you have the wrong number."

CHAPTER 23

Let Heaven and Nature Sing

We are compounded of dust and the light of a star.

—Loren Eiseley

THE OTHER DAY I was speaking to an audience at Grace Cathedral, the Episcopal church atop Nob Hill in San Francisco, and a very young woman asked me, "What level of hope do you allow yourself?"

I thought this was a strange question from one so young. She should have been outside. It was a sunny day, and inside she had to put up with me.

I told her I allowed very little else but hope. If I allowed myself to give up on hope, I would just have to order a Tanqueray martini—straight up, no distractions—then another and another.

She was young. She did not laugh.

Look, I said, every time you see a child come and begin to walk and learn how to talk, there it is: hope. There is this enormous

capability within all of us. We keep producing it, again and again, as a species. I have hope, I said, that we will stop smothering the genius of children. What gives them a chance to blossom? *Being outdoors.* You don't get much feeling for history, for the Earth, when you spend twelve years in a concrete box trying to get educated. Under those conditions, what you become educated about are concrete boxes.

Learn to read the Earth, as Father Thomas Berry says.

A cobweb in the attic gathers dust, and is ugly. But a cobweb outdoors gathers dewdrops that scintillate in the sun. Get out. Find your hope. Read the Earth. It is an extraordinary book: full color, stereo sound, wonderful aromas, the wind. It is an extraordinary planet.

You ask me how much hope I allow myself. I get my hope when I say: Look at that living thing.

Look at mountains, also.

Notice the way rivers meander, when they need to.

I myself would like to return to the time of Moses and ask him to go back up the mountain and bring down the other tablet. The problem with the Ten Commandments is that they only talk of how we're supposed to treat each other. There's not a bloody word about how we're supposed to treat the Earth. Well, we don't and won't have each other without the Earth, and we are losing it. That other tablet must be up on the mountain still. Moses must have dropped it. Find that other tablet.

In Genesis 1:28, God tells the newly created Eve and Adam: "Be fruitful, and multiply, and replenish the earth, and subdue it:

and have dominion over the fish of the sea, and over the fowl of the air, and over every living thing that moveth upon the earth."

As Wallace Stegner put it in *Where the Bluebird Sings to the Lemonade Springs*, "Whether or not God meant it in quite that way, and whether or not men translated Him correctly, many used these words as justification to make the Earth serve human purposes alone."

John Widtsoe, a Mormon patriarch in the American West, put it most bluntly: "The destiny of man is to possess the whole Earth; the destiny of the Earth is to be subject to man. There can be no full conquest of the Earth, and no real satisfaction to humanity, if large portions of the Earth remain beyond his highest control."

In another essay, Stegner commented upon Widtsoe's witlessness: "That doctrine offends me to the bottom of my not-very-Christian soul."

I agree.

Stegner was zeroing in on that word "subdue." Some scholarly friends of mine maintain that the original meaning was "steward" the Earth. Think of the difference a one-word injunction makes, over 2,000 years. For the future, let's try "protect."

Genesis was probably written when the population of the Earth was 50 million. Jesus Christ was born when the population was about 200 million. It is quite a different ball game, these days, when the population is 5.6 billion, and we're using up those fish and their seas, those fowl and the air they fly through, and every living thing—including the cattle and the soil and streamsides they trample.

Isaiah had the right idea, if we are interpreting him properly, when he said: "Woe unto them that join house to house, that lay field to field, till there be no place, that they may be placed alone in the midst of the earth!"

To me, God and Nature are synonymous, and neither could wait the billions of years before man arrived to decide what to look like. I hear that two scientists were discussing the big bang, and God, leaning over their shoulders, asked, "Which big bang?" I have as much trouble comprehending Creation as I do comprehending what it was created out of. I like mystery, the unending search for truth, the truth of beauty. I would have no use for pearly gates and streets of gold if canyon wrens were not admitted.

CHAPTER 24

For Those Who Would Save the Earth

Whatever you can do, or dream you can, begin it.
Boldness has genius, power and magic in it.
— Johann Wolfgang von Goethe

IN *The Scottish Himalayan Expedition*, mountaineer William H. Murray reflected on the organization and will-power necessary to begin the expedition:

> Until one is committed there is hesitancy, the chance to draw back, always ineffectiveness. Concerning all acts of initiative (and creation), there is one elementary truth, the ignorance of which kills countless ideas and splendid plans: that the moment one definitely commits oneself, then Providence moves, too. All sorts of things occur to help one that would never otherwise have occurred. A whole stream of events issues from the decision, raising in one's favour all manner of unforeseen incidents and

mectings and material assistance, which no man could have dreamt would have come his way.

In the not-so-distant past, I saw Murray's remark on commitment serve almost as religion for the people, including me, who helped keep dams out of Dinosaur National Monument, the Yukon, and the Grand Canyon, who helped keep loggers with itchy axes out of Olympic National Park; who helped ban DDT; who helped establish the National Wilderness Preservation System and additions to the National Park System in the North Cascades, Kings Canyon, the Redwoods, Great Basin, at Point Reyes, the Golden Gate, Cape Cod, Fire Island.

We helped do all this with a Sierra Club membership less than one-tenth of its present size. Even our success in gaining passage of the Alaska National Interest Lands Conservation Act of 1980 was accomplished with a far smaller club than now exists.

Back then the Sierra Club made all this possible by boldly asserting itself. It took the words of John Muir to heart: "Climb the mountains and get their good tidings."

There are now millions of dues-paying environmentalists in the United States alone. Some count the number at 10 million. There are more; they just haven't signed up yet. But whatever the number, they don't seem to have anywhere near the power they should.

What are the reasons for this? The quick and dirty answer is: lack of boldness, smug leadership, battles over turf, absence from the legislative arena, bureaucracy, and no fun.

LET'S START by talking about Benton MacKaye's Theory of How to Build Big by Starting Small. Benton MacKaye was the father—the conceptualizer—of the Appalachian Trail. He was the first person, that I know of, to conceive of an organized wilderness system. He liked to come south to Washington, D.C., to escape the rigors of a Boston winter, and he would stay at the Cosmos Club, which had been started by John Wesley Powell with an eye toward bringing science to the attention of Congress. Benton was in his eighties when we began our chats, and he had another decade of wisdom ahead of him.

"If you want an organization of cannibals," Benton would say, "then only cannibals may be admitted." He would pause while you took in the import of that remark. Here's what he meant:

In the beginning get only the people who think the way you do, who believe. Put your act together with them, and make the idea and the organization as strong as you can, before you launch it to the public. This is the way to build an organization with real power.

Make it very clear what the organization stands for. Let that be known, and let that be the welcome mat for anyone who wants to come under your tent.

If you start worrying from the outset about pleasing too much or offending certain people or certain groups, then you're already lost. You've got to let people know you are not going to sell out, that you are not going to waffle on the basic principles. You can say, "I haven't reached all my conclusions yet; I may not be all that practical. But this is the way I think it ought to be, and we stand for that." Then see who joins and what happens.

On the other hand, I don't believe in purity. That's another mistake. It is ironic, but being too pure is about the same as being too practical. Practical people have made all their decisions, as I said a bit earlier. They have lost the ability to listen, and are determined to repeat the errors of their ancestors. Purists are just practical people who have gone even further than necessary.

Once the organization is off the ground, don't be so quick to take credit for every victory. That's the time to work on coalition building. Howard Zahniser didn't seek to have The Wilderness Society take credit for everything, even when it could have. Again and again he would say, They did it, those other people. He gave other groups the credit. The idea is not to claim turf. The idea is to save turf. How do we build a constituency for the Earth?

If your purism consists of love for life and for the only planet we know to have life on it, I'll accept that. But don't then say you've got to love it in the following manner, and by the numbers. Love it your own way, and if you have a better way, please tell me about it.

The modern environmental movement seems to be having trouble with leadership. Who are the leaders? Where is the charisma? Environmental groups go to Hollywood to find a sympathetic celebrity to provide them with glitz. Where are our own charismatic leaders, whom the media would want to quote directly?

I learned a lot about leadership on the early Sierra Club High Trips. These trips were set up by John Muir and attorney Will Colby to get people into the wilderness where they could have fun and fall in love with the wild. It was a simple strategy. They did fall in love with the mountains, and many of these people went on to lead corporations, become artists and writers, and move in political circles. They never forgot the wilderness.

There were mules and camp fires on the High Trips, lots of stories and laughter, sometimes up to two hundred people on the same four-week outing. I was the leader in 1939—1941 and again in 1946—1956. You had to be the benign dictator. If you asked everybody individually where they wanted to camp the next day, you'd have chaos. Perhaps the leaders could have taken a different trail or climbed toward a different pass, but this would have had to be determined earlier, when the logistics were worked out.

We were open at the planning stage, but once we got started, we would say: Have a good time, take all the detours you want, walk with your own friends. You don't have to go in lockstep. But here is where we are camping at the end of the day, at the

foot of Tilden Lake, or wherever, because that's where the supplies will be, and dinner.

We couldn't have people all over the mountain. It would have been unsafe and increased the trip's impact on the mountain.

One of the reasons certain groups don't work too well, as of yet, is that they are so busy looking for consensus and fighting hierarchy that they miss the forests *and* the trees. Too much consensus makes it too easy for the lowest common denominator to rule. The group is not going to get "felled in."

That's what Cpl. Wid Corn used to say when I was in the Tenth Mountain Division. "Come on, you guys, quit melling around and get felled in."

That is what's happening with the Green Party. They are melling around and not getting felled in. They argue. They argue some more. They agonize about hierarchy. They don't want to offend anyone. But they disdain having character. They don't seem to want to let anybody lead, and leaders are necessary.

How far can you extend this concept? Not too far. The danger comes when someone tries to say: This is the way it is, and I'm the leader, and I am going to continue to be the leader, and don't anybody get in my way. It is very important that leadership change.

Once in a while (a great while) I'm grateful the Sierra Club didn't want me to be its executive director forever. That was a good thing for all hands, although I didn't feel so good about it at the time.

I like to pose this question: What do environmentalists, feminists, the far-righteous, the right-to-lifers, and the Bible have in common? Answer: No humor. No one has disagreed yet.

Of course, maybe we need two Green Parties, the light green and the dark green. That is, Republican and Democrat, conservative and progressive. The environmental movement needs to be much more a part of political discussion in this country. This was the reason I founded the League of Conservation Voters, so that we could see who was voting on the side of the Earth, and who was out there trashing it.

By whatever means, we need to send a message: It would be nice to make a new try at practicing democracy.

HOW DO YOU bring politicians onto the side of saving the Earth? The first thing you do is show them what they are saving, as we did on those High Trips, or as John Muir did when he camped in Yosemite with President Theodore Roosevelt. Roosevelt went away rhapsodizing about natural cathedrals. Back in Washington, he helped to protect a great deal of wilderness from those in his own party who wanted to scalp, pulp, and package everything that lay between the cities. They did a pretty good job of that in Michigan, Wisconsin, Oregon, and Washington, in Roosevelt's time. At the rim of the Grand Canyon, he could say, "Leave it as it is. The ages have been at work on it, and man can only mar it."

Roosevelt didn't need much convincing. At a time when he was severely depressed, after his wife and daughter had tragically

and suddenly died, he came to the Badlands of the Dakotas and Montana with the idea of healing himself in wildness. When he left that open prairie life and returned to politics, he knew what had saved him, and he knew it was what could save the country, and all of us.

Representative John Saylor of Pennsylvania started out as a conservative Republican, too. America's wild rivers, rather than our wild prairie, influenced him. Many politicians yearn to have structures built in their names, but John Saylor didn't build a monument. He saved one: Dinosaur National Monument.

In the early 1950s the Bureau of Reclamation and its water-greedy supporters, who wanted the Echo Park and Split Mountain dams built in the Upper Colorado Basin, put out that anyone who considered rafting the Yampa or Green rivers must possess a severe death wish. This was in the days before millions of young Americans reclaimed our wilderness with rafts, kayaks, horses, llamas, and high-tech shoes.

John Saylor decided to go out and look at what he would be voting to flood (or cut)—something not enough senators and members of Congress are willing to do. He brought along his son, and also Joseph W. Penfold, who was the solemnly humorous Western leader of the Izaak Walton League. Penfold brought his son, too. It was Joe who once said, "The engineers in the Bureau of Reclamation are like beavers. They can't stand the sight of running water." Joe, John, and the two sons got their feet wet on the Yampa, and that's not all. Saylor returned to Congress a bull-dog for wilderness.

When we were being badgered by the House Committee on Interior and Insular Affairs, a group of gentlemen who could never understand how anything could ever take precedence over the orderly eradication of wilderness, John would save us. His voice would rise, stentorian vibrations rumbled, his usually amused countenance turned stern, and soon he was plucking information from commissioners, secretaries, and agency technicians that the bureaucrats did not want out. John Saylor learned to spot rapids on the Green. When he got back to Washington, he spotted truth-substitutes, which is what antienvironmental bureaucrats used to like to spread before they spread disinformation.

There are bureaucrats in the environmental movement, too. The cure for them is the same as it is for politicians: Get out of Washington (or San Francisco, New York, Los Angeles) and listen to the mountains. Float the rivers. It is too easy to lose touch with the grass, with the grass roots. Don't ever give up what you haven't seen.

And don't be unwilling to make yourself a little unpopular by trying to protect something that people want to unprotect.

Some environmentalists will do anything to preserve their access, imagined or real, to power.

I once had an illuminating conversation with John Baker, who was then president of the National Audubon Society. John Baker told me that Harold Ickes, who was Franklin Roosevelt's Secretary of the Interior and one of the greatest, had complained to him that he was "having some trouble with your Audubon

ladies in the Southeast." They were concerned about threats to the ivory-billed woodpecker. Baker told the "Audubon ladies" to go easy, which they did.

"After that," John told me, "I never had trouble getting an appointment with Harold Ickes."

But the ivory-billed woodpecker is extinct.

Access to power is good. It makes things easier when a Bob Marshall is running the recreation division of the Forest Service or a Hazel O'Leary is Secretary of Energy instead of a Dixy Lee Ray. But when access is not there, as it rarely was during the Reagan administration, we still have our recourse: boycotts, voting, the truth, the courts, and the strong desire of most Americans to drink clean water, to have their children breathe clean air, and to have their grandchildren experience what it means to be able to walk beyond the roads.

You can never tell when a slight push in the right direction will move politicians who want to be moved or who make up their own minds from time to time. President Jimmy Carter had a dozen of us in the White House to explain, among other things, why he could not veto legislation authorizing the Clinch River Breeder Reactor—bad nuclear news. Before departing, I handed him a letter signed by me but written by Jeff Knight, Friends of the Earth's energy expert in Washington. In one page plus four lines, Jeff explained why the president should veto the bill and what the consequences would be.

Having already explained why he couldn't, Jimmy Carter did.

Moral 1: Write a good letter—and hand-carry it!

Moral 2: Thank your benefactor.

I met again with Jimmy Carter, when he was no longer president. It was the day the reactivated Tenth Mountain Division, my old outfit, arrived peacefully on Haiti. Were it not for Carter's intervention the day before, many Americans and Haitians would already have been dead and many more about to be.

By the simple expedient of trying to be fair, Carter got the U.S. out of a rut, just as he had a few months earlier in North Korea. Carter is a president, wrongly abused by the media, who has managed to recreate himself in a short space of time. I was reminded that war is the ultimate environmental disaster and that Carter had managed to avert disaster twice in one year. I smiled at the irony that so many pundits, ever ready to heap abuse on President Clinton at the sight of the first body bag bringing a Tenth Mountain man home, would be furious at President Carter for denying them that opportunity. I guess peace is simply too dull for some members of the media to endure.

Part of the problem, too, is that the haves of the world are still treating the have-nots as the colonies of old were treated, and this has a bad effect upon what irreplaceable wilderness we have left. The haves lend money to the erstwhile colonies, insisting that most of what they lend be spent at the source, in the donor country. To pay back the loan, the have-nots invest in cash crops for the haves, produced most abundantly on their best land. That forces them into the poorer soil of their wildlands in order to

produce food for their own subsistence. Where rain forests exist, they become early victims. The forests are logged for cash, then replaced by cattle, also sold for cash—and also maintaining high cholesterol levels in their high-living customers.

Thus, the haves are destroying wilderness by ricochet.

In 1994, at a meeting of the Canadian Environmental Network (a network of some 1,800 organizations) in Ottawa, Brian Staszinski and I launched the idea of forming the Ecological Council of the Americas. There isn't anything modest about the name, but then a certain amount of boldness is required to counteract what we see wrong with NAFTA, the North American Free Trade Agreement. What we see wrong is the implication that there must be no environmental barriers to North American trade. What we see right is that there must be no trade barriers to achieving a sustainable environment, without which there can be no trade at all.

We forget that we are all in this together, the haves and the have-nots.

I once asked William Reilly, appointed by President George H. W. Bush to direct the Environmental Protection Agency, what the flowers-to-brickbats ratio was during his term. He answered by quoting his predecessor, William Ruckelshaus: "The day you come and the day you leave, you get flowers. All the rest of the time it rains."

Randy Hayes, of the Rainforest Action Network, thinks environmentalists can sometimes be overly preoccupied with access because so many lawyers came into the movement in the

1980s. Lawyers are by nature negotiators, and this, thinks Randy, led to some trade-offs with things like the North American Free Trade Agreement and with GATT (General Agreement on Tariffs and Trade).

I have great respect for lawyers, however, so long as they've all gone through some sort of therapy.

Lawyers elect to be schizo. They choose to represent a John Muir on one case and a Rush Limbaugh on another. They are like the man who said, "I'm trying to follow the teachings of Jesus Christ and Mephistopheles, and I'm having problems."

In the late 1940s a lawyer told me, "Nature has no rights." He was wrong. More recent lawyers now allow the Earth its rights.

Lawyers stopped the Storm King pumped-storage hydropower scheme on the Hudson River. Lawsuits stopped the dewatering of Mono Lake by the City of Los Angeles. They have begun the process of saving the ancient forests of the Northwest by showing a federal judge, a staunch Reagan appointee, how federal agencies like the Forest Service have engaged in a pattern of lawlessness in willfully giving away, at a fraction of its value, the public treasure to timber companies, and endangering the Endangered Species Act in regard to the spotted owl. Lawyers have become invaluable. I like a full arsenal.

OF COURSE, I never wanted a level playing field. I'm a mountaineer.

I don't always like to win. Some lessons are better learned the other way. Losing can demonstrate the need for reform—and a

new way of achieving it. The way you learn not to touch a hot stove is by touching it.

Many environmental organizations are not operating on a level playing field because their tax-deductible status prevents their lobbying vigorously enough and forbids their being political. The Sierra Club does not have this problem since, as one of my finer acts, I lost the club its tax-deductible status in the Grand Canyon battle.

We saved the Grand Canyon. Who gives a damn whether your yearly dues are deductible? Nobody. By not being deductible, the organization can support direct political activity.

I have been preaching for a long time that deductible environmental organizations need a separate corporation that functions as a nondeductible associate. Decisions are made by an independent board, funds are never commingled, but there is a continuity of mission, and there can be enough overlap of directors, under current tax law, to make that independence and continuity possible.

I should add that I got the tax-deductible Sierra Club Foundation under way six years before the IRS attacked the club. This attack produced a big surge in club membership, in the same way that James Watt's flop as secretary of the interior under President Reagan brought as many as a million new recruits to the environmental cause.

The head of one effective environmental organization separates those who would like to join the movement to save the Earth,

but who are doing nothing, into three groups: those who need direction, those who need motivation, and those who have just plain given up. So many people want to help if only given a chance.

Look at MBAs, whom many might consider a hard choice for environmental recruitment. But MBAs need to learn what their talents are for. What they are learning is how to cash in faster. That's not even for the birds. They should be learning what it costs to fail to lead us into a sustainable society.

We've got great things to do. Life is a school of opportunities. (Don't call them problems.) Some people just need to become excited. They need to learn that they can change things.

I get these letters from old people's organizations that are concerned about entitlements: "You made these investments. Now you deserve all the stuff back." I want my age-mates—those who are not dead—to think about something else besides their entitlements. What have they cost the Earth, during their time on it? What can they pay *back* now? Not with a lot of money, but with their energy buttressed by the wisdom they have accumulated. This is another opportunity for them. It'll make them a lot happier to think about fixing up the Earth than it will to ruminate upon their ailments.

In our society old people are put out to pasture. I don't believe in pasteurized elders. I would remind them that Theodore Roosevelt said, "It is better to wear out than to rust out."

The trick is to move my contemporaries around and aim them in the right direction.

Wallace Stegner used to say, "Walk softly and break no twigs." That may have been what he thought he was best at. Myself, I've always been a twig breaker. If the twigs are breaking and you hear the sound, you wake up to the fact that there's an opportunity. You try to work out a deal with reasonable people who aren't breaking twigs. Walking in bear country, it's better to break twigs than to surprise a bear because you didn't.

I once ran a piece of Stegner's called the "The Battle Between the Cowboys and the Bird Watchers" in the *Sierra Club Bulletin*. *Harper's* magazine had not accepted it. At the end, Stegner quoted Senator Arthur Watkins of Utah, who asked: "Why don't you have wilderness near the cities where more people can use it?" Stegner answered, "It was not given to man to create wilderness, but he can create deserts, and has."

Stegner, long a Sierra Club friend, wrote a devastating letter in the fracas that led to my walking the plank as executive director. He accused me of having been "bitten by the worm of power." More people remember that than his apology. So I say to the heads of environmental organizations: If you are going to get into fights, avoid people who happen to be extraordinarily articulate. They say strong things they may not quite mean just because that's the way they say anything. If you have to get into a fight with a master, make sure he or she stutters.

When Stegner's piece was typeset, I needed to shorten a few lines for the printer by getting rid of the widows and orphans, dangling words at the tops and bottoms of columns. You couldn't

do that to Stegner's copy. There was inevitability in what he'd written. You couldn't add a word or take a word away. It was right. I began to wonder, how the hell did they get rid of the orphans and widows in the Bible?

We've lost some of those literary champions of wilderness and the environment. When you have photographers like Ansel Adams and Eliot Porter, and writers like Wallace Stegner, Loren Eiseley, Nancy Newhall, and Rachel Carson appearing in an organization's magazine and publishing books under the environmental banner, the high ground is easily captured. Those special books won many of our battles for us, sitting there on the coffee tables until people of great power looked into them and began to understand. Truth and beauty can still win battles. We need more art, more passion, more wit in defense of the Earth.

I THINK the real reason I was fired in 1969 after seventeen years as executive director of the Sierra Club was my opposition to developing nuclear power at Diablo Canyon in California. Until that moment, my other faults, which were beyond number, were tolerated, even forgiven. Then suddenly I was like Clark Kerr, president of the University of California from 1958 to 1967, who said, "I came to my job the same way I left it—fired with enthusiasm."

You must have an instinct for the future, if you are to lead environmental organizations. Nuclear power is not in the best interests of the future of this planet. Alan Watts once told me, "A star

is a planet on which intelligent beings experimented with atomic power." Last year, architect William McDonough told a group of us, "In the last few decades, the U.S. has spent half a trillion dollars subsidizing something nobody wants—radioactivity."

At times you need to take some risks to save the future. Pacific Gas & Electric must regret it took the risk I warned against—the threat to the future. The power company blithely told its rate-payers that the Diablo Canyon nuclear reactors would cost less than $400 million. So far, PG&E has spent $5 billion and counting, and decommissioning looms ahead, as an added, unknown, potentially disastrous expense.

Taking risks has been my trouble in the environmental movement. Because I was a climber, I am aware that there's a certain amount of danger in getting off level ground. When you get up to where the holds are very thin and there's a great deal of air under your feet, you know that it's not a good time to slip because you might not survive it. Perhaps that is why I have always liked this quotation: "A ship in harbor is safe, but that's not what ships were built for." I like to get out of port. I think we were built to explore.

I have my regrets. I regret having hurt people. In the thick of things, you can become abrasive. Once a friend was working me over on budgetary matters, or I thought he was. He said, "I'm only trying to protect you." I reacted angrily, and said, "You protect me with the back of your hand."

I hurt him, and had not meant to. That flip statement did not